BASIC / NOT BORING
MATH SKILLS

GEOMETRY &
MEASUREMENT

Grades 6–8⁺

Inventive Exercises to Sharpen
Skills and Raise Achievement

Series Concept & Development
by Imogene Forte & Marjorie Frank
Exercises by Terri Breeden

Incentive Publications, Inc.
Nashville, Tennessee

About the cover:
Bound resist, or tie dye, is the most ancient known method of fabric surface design. The brilliance of the basic tie dye design on this cover reflects the possibilities that emerge from the mastery of basic skills.

Illustrated by Kathleen Bullock
Cover art by Mary Patricia Deprez, dba Tye Dye Mary®
Cover design by Marta Drayton, Joe Shibley, and W. Paul Nance
Edited by Anna Quinn

ISBN 0-86530-367-3

PRINTED IN THE UNITED STATES OF AMERICA

TABLE OF CONTENTS

CELEBRATE BASIC MATH SKILLS

Basic does not mean boring! There certainly is nothing dull about . . .

   . . . finding out about legends and traditions in the Olympics

   . . . measuring the sizes of tracks for a dozen different sports

   . . . learning who's broken which Olympic records

   . . . calculating the weight of a gold medal

   . . . getting to know facts about Olympic athletes from Hercules to Shannon Miller

   . . . figuring out how fast Michael Johnson really ran

   . . . examining Olympic history to find that the first weights were actually boulders and that early yacht sails were bedspreads

The idea of celebrating the basics is just what it sounds like—enjoying and developing the basic skills of geometry and measurement. The pages that follow are full of exercises for students that will help to review and strengthen specific, basic skills in the content area of math. This is not just any ordinary "fill-in-the-blanks" way to learn. The high-interest activities will put students to work applying a rich variety of the most important skills and strategies for working with geometric figures and for measuring. Kids will do this work while learning some fascinating facts about the Summer Olympic Games and enjoying challenging adventures with sports-related dilemmas.

The pages in this book can be used in many ways . . .

   . . . for individual students to sharpen a particular skill

   . . . with a small group needing to relearn or sharpen a skill

   . . . as an instructional tool for teaching a skill to any size group

   . . . by students working on their own

   . . . by students working under the direction of an adult.

Each page may be used to introduce a new skill or set of math facts, reinforce a skill, or even to assess a student's ability to perform a skill. And, there's more than just the 40 pages of great student activities! You'll also find a hearty appendix of resources helpful for students and teachers—including a ready-to-use test for assessing geometry and measurement content skills.

As students take on the challenges of these adventures with geometry and measurement, they will sharpen their mastery of basic skills, and will enjoy learning to the fullest. And as you watch them check off the basic math skills they've strengthened, you can celebrate with them!

SKILLS CHECKLIST FOR GEOMETRY & MEASUREMENT

✔	SKILL	PAGE(S)
	Identify and describe points, lines, and planes	10
	Identify kinds of angles	11, 27, 43
	Identify kinds of lines	10, 12, 13
	Identify and define kinds of triangles	16
	Identify and define different polygons	14, 15, 16
	Identify, define, and distinguish among quadrilaterals	17, 23, 25
	Define and determine perimeter	18, 19, 40
	Identify properties and parts of a circle	20
	Determine the circumference of circles	21
	Identify similar and congruent figures	22, 28
	Use formulas to determine the area of quadrilaterals	23, 40
	Use a formula to determine the area of triangles	24, 40
	Use a formula to determine the area of trapezoids	25, 40
	Use a formula to determine the area of circles	26
	Identify congruent angles	27
	Identify congruent triangles and other polygons	28
	Recognize and define different space figures	29
	Use formulas to determine volume of space figures	29, 30, 31, 42
	Use formulas to determine the volume of prisms and pyramids	30, 31, 42
	Identify and use various metric units for measuring	32, 33
	Convert among metric measurements	33
	Identify and use various U.S. customary units for measuring	34, 35, 36
	Convert among U.S. measurements	34, 35, 36
	Determine the appropriate unit for a measurement task	34, 37
	Measure length	38, 39
	Measure and find area	40
	Find weight	41
	Measure and find volume	42
	Measure angles	43
	Estimate measurements	44-45
	Convert U.S. customary units to metric units	34, 46
	Determine measurements of temperature	47
	Solve problems with time measurements	48

GEOMETRY & MEASUREMENT

Skills Exercises

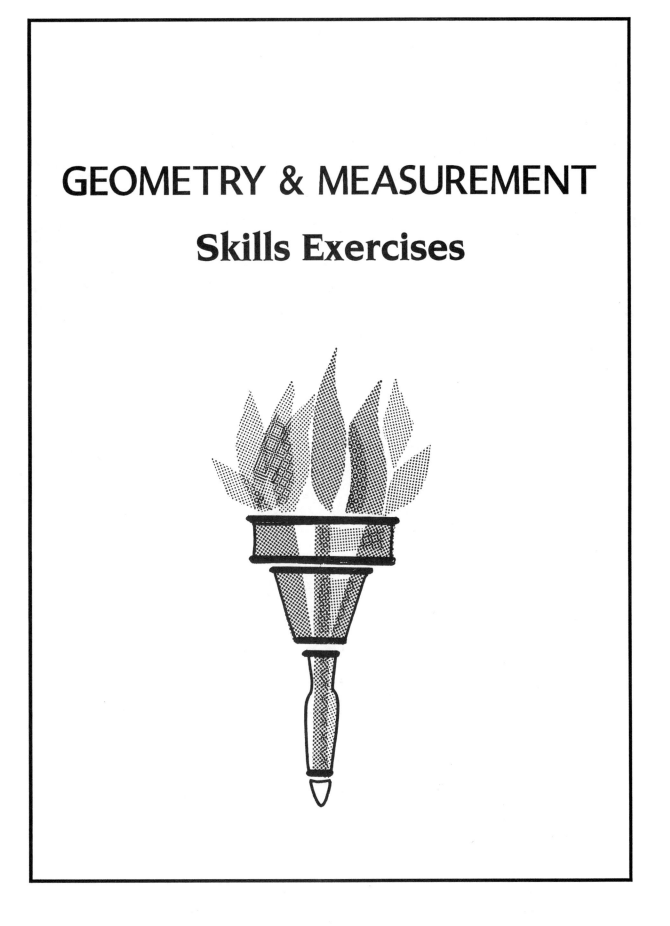

FLYING FEATHERS

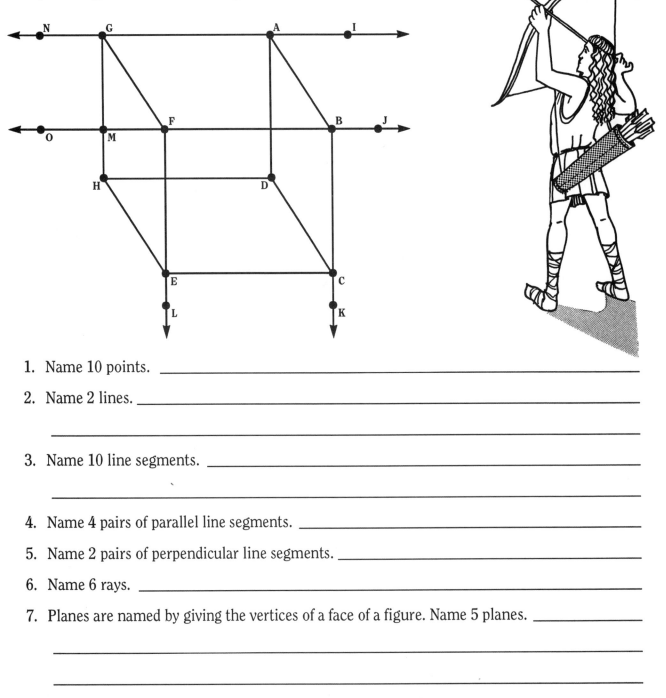

There is an Olympic legend that Hercules, an archer, founded the Olympic games. Instead of shooting arrows into a target, ancient archers used live tethered doves as their targets. Using birds as targets gave birth to the saying, "Now the feathers are really flying!" Check your aim with the following problems.

Study the diagram and answer the questions below.

1. Name 10 points. _____

2. Name 2 lines. _____

_____

3. Name 10 line segments. _____

_____

4. Name 4 pairs of parallel line segments. _____

5. Name 2 pairs of perpendicular line segments. _____

6. Name 6 rays. _____

7. Planes are named by giving the vertices of a face of a figure. Name 5 planes. _____

_____

_____

Name _____

SOME SPECTACULAR ANGLES

Gymnasts get their bodies into the most spectacular positions. If you watch them, you'll see all kinds of angles represented in their maneuvers.

A. Identify the numbered angle of each gymnast's body as **acute, obtuse,** or **right**.

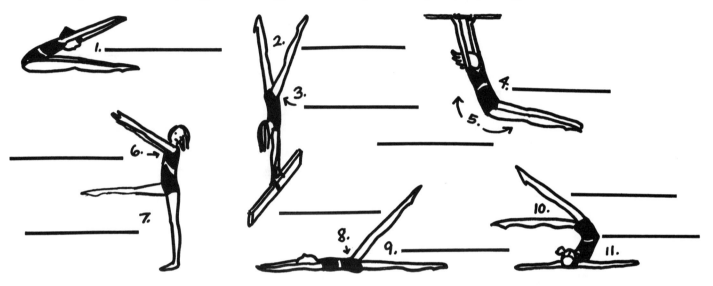

B. Identify these angles as either **complementary** or **supplementary** angles. Then find the measure of each numbered angle.

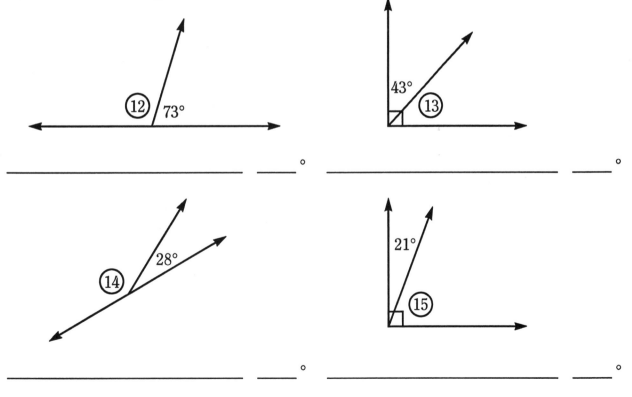

Name _____

CONFUSION IN THE VILLAGE

Pierre could not find his way around the Olympic Village so he asked for directions. Use the map to determine where Pierre will be if he follows these directions.

1. Pierre left his room in International Dorm A through the front door on a street that runs parallel to 3rd Avenue. He turned at the intersection of 1st Street and Elm Street. Where was he going?

    _____

2. Pierre was exercising at the Training Gym. He was on Broad Street and turned left at the intersection of Broad and 5th. Where did he go?

    _____

3. Siam told Pierre that the ATM machine was on a street parallel to 8th Street. What street was Siam referring to? _____

4. Pierre was running late. Write the best directions from International Dorm A to the Bus Stop. Use the words *intersection* and *parallel* in your directions.

    _____

    _____

    _____

    _____

5. If Pierre was at the Track and Field area and he exited at the 8th Street exit and turned at the intersection of 8th and N. West Boulevard, where would he be?_____

6. Pierre attended morning worship at the church. He walked on Church Street and turned right on a street that ran parallel to 8th Street. Then he went approximately two blocks and entered an establishment and bought a soft drink. Where was he?_____

7. Andrea told Pierre that 8th Street runs perpendicular to N. West Boulevard. Is that true or false? _____

8. Romana told Pierre that the laundry is just past the intersection of 1st Street and Broad Street. Is that true or false?_____

9. Pierre told Mary Ann that the Oak Street and Annex do not intersect. Is this true or false? __

10. Pierre needed to go from the pool to the training gym. Write directions below. Be certain to use words like *perpendicular, parallel,* and *intersecting* in your directions.

    _____

    _____

    _____

Use with map on page 13.

Name

12

CONFUSION IN THE VILLAGE, CONTINUED

Use with page 12.

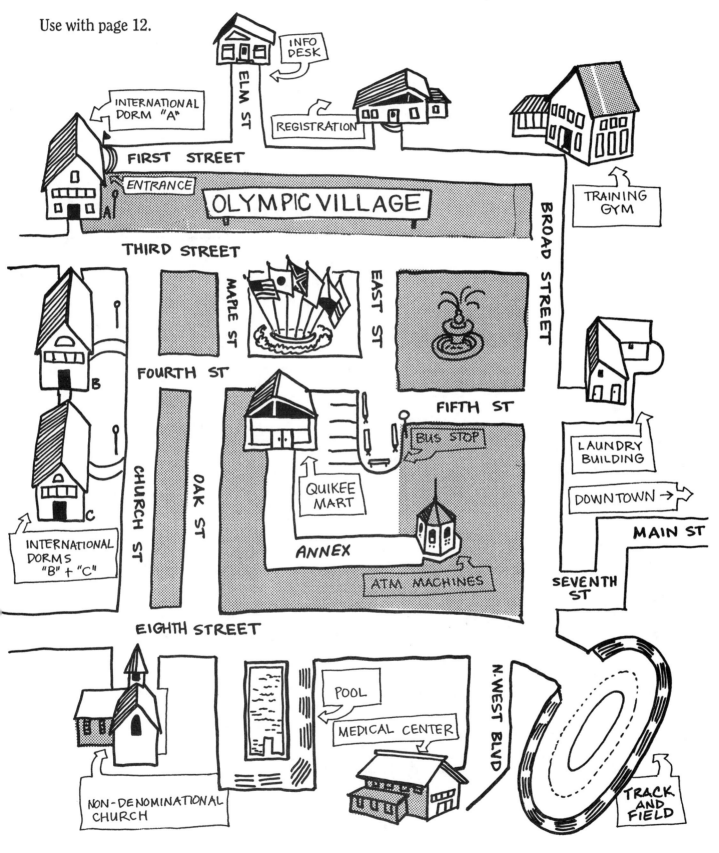

THE COLORS OF THE OLYMPICS

At the opening ceremonies of the Olympics, Tasha was awed by the beautiful, colorful flags. She had never guessed that flags could be so different! Match her written descriptions of the flags to the drawings on the next page. Write the name of the country's flag after each description.

1. One strikingly beautiful flag contained 1 triangle, 2 trapezoids of different colors, and 1 pentagon. Country _____

2. Another one caught my eye because it had a dodecagon and 4 rectangles. Country _____

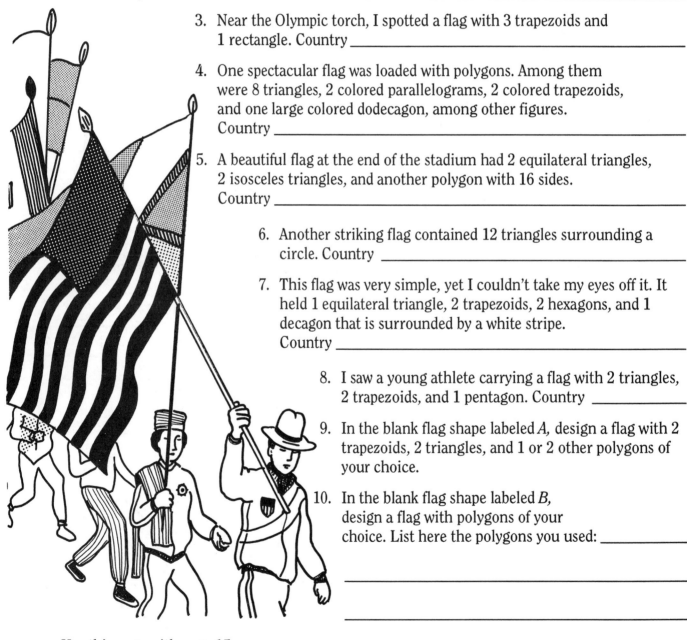

3. Near the Olympic torch, I spotted a flag with 3 trapezoids and 1 rectangle. Country _____

4. One spectacular flag was loaded with polygons. Among them were 8 triangles, 2 colored parallelograms, 2 colored trapezoids, and one large colored dodecagon, among other figures. Country _____

5. A beautiful flag at the end of the stadium had 2 equilateral triangles, 2 isosceles triangles, and another polygon with 16 sides. Country _____

6. Another striking flag contained 12 triangles surrounding a circle. Country _____

7. This flag was very simple, yet I couldn't take my eyes off it. It held 1 equilateral triangle, 2 trapezoids, 2 hexagons, and 1 decagon that is surrounded by a white stripe. Country _____

8. I saw a young athlete carrying a flag with 2 triangles, 2 trapezoids, and 1 pentagon. Country _____

9. In the blank flag shape labeled A, design a flag with 2 trapezoids, 2 triangles, and 1 or 2 other polygons of your choice.

10. In the blank flag shape labeled B, design a flag with polygons of your choice. List here the polygons you used: _____

_____

_____

Use this page with page 15.

Name

14

THE COLORS OF THE OLYMPICS, CONTINUED

Use with page 14.

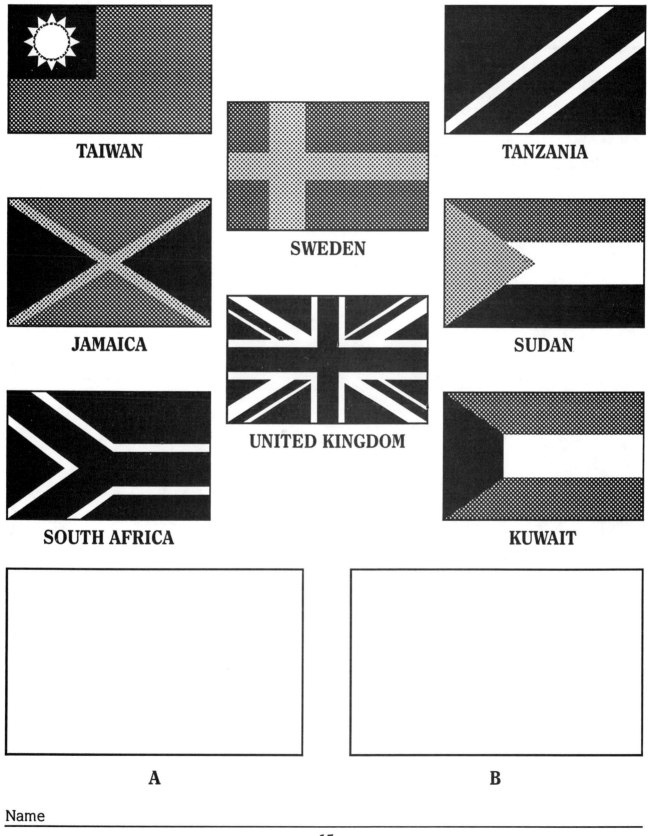

TAIWAN

TANZANIA

SWEDEN

JAMAICA

SUDAN

UNITED KINGDOM

SOUTH AFRICA

KUWAIT

A

B

Name

POOLSIDE GEOMETRY

One of the Olympic Pools that Kendall used in competition had an unusual and spectacular tile mosaic bottom. Identify the triangles and other figures by coloring them according to the key below.

blue = scalene triangles
red = equilateral triangles
green = isosceles triangles
black = right triangles
yellow = other shapes

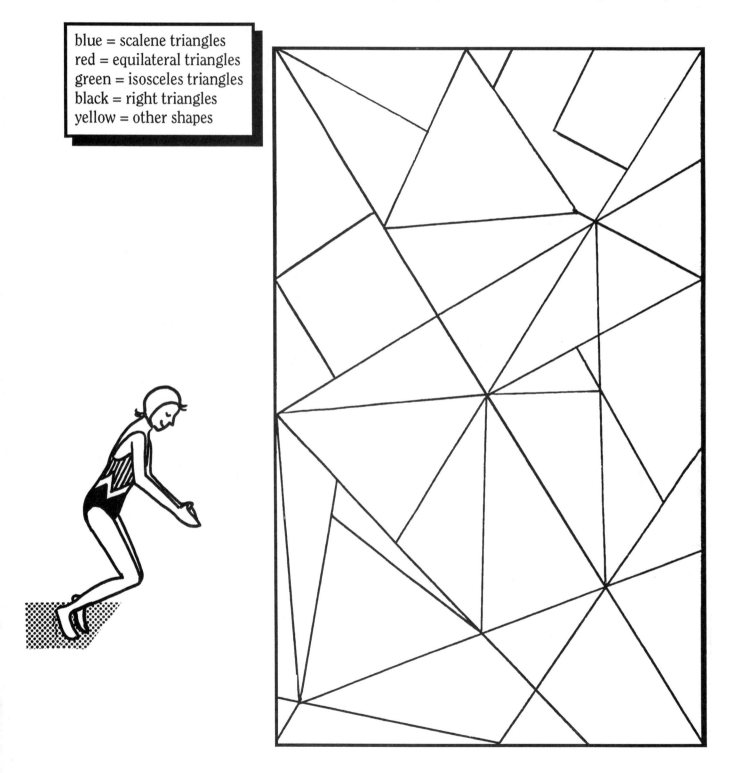

Name

DIFFERENT—YET THE SAME

The Olympic Games capture attention like no other sporting event. An estimated 35 billion people watch this international competition. The Olympics bring together people from almost 200 different countries. The athletes and fans share the common interest in the sports contests, but they represent widely diverse backgrounds. The shapes you run into at the Olympics are just as diverse, even if they share common characteristics. Many of them are quadrilaterals (4-sided polygons) yet the quadrilaterals differ.

A.

Match these different quadrilaterals with their correct definitions.

_____ 1. parallelogram   A. a parallelogram with all sides and angles congruent

_____ 2. trapezoid   B. a quadrilateral with exactly one pair of parallel sides

_____ 3. rectangle   C. a parallelogram with all angles congruent

_____ 4. rhombus   D. a parallelogram with all sides congruent

_____ 5. square   E. a quadrilateral with two pairs of parallel sides

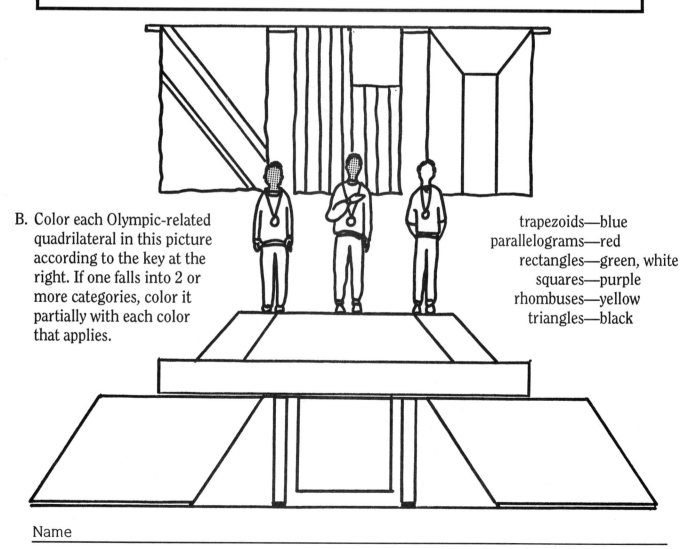

B. Color each Olympic-related quadrilateral in this picture according to the key at the right. If one falls into 2 or more categories, color it partially with each color that applies.

trapezoids—blue
parallelograms—red
rectangles—green, white
squares—purple
rhombuses—yellow
triangles—black

Name

TRACKING DOWN DISTANCES

Athletes at the Summer Olympics run, ride, practice, and compete on many different tracks, surfaces, and courses. Calculate how far it is around the outside edge (perimeter) of each of these sports surfaces.

Use with page 19.

Name

TRACKING DOWN DISTANCES, CONTINUED

Use with page 18.

Rectangle	P = 2 (l + w)
Square, rhombus	P = 4 s
Triangle	P = s + s + s
Circle	P = π d
Other Polygons	P = sum of sides

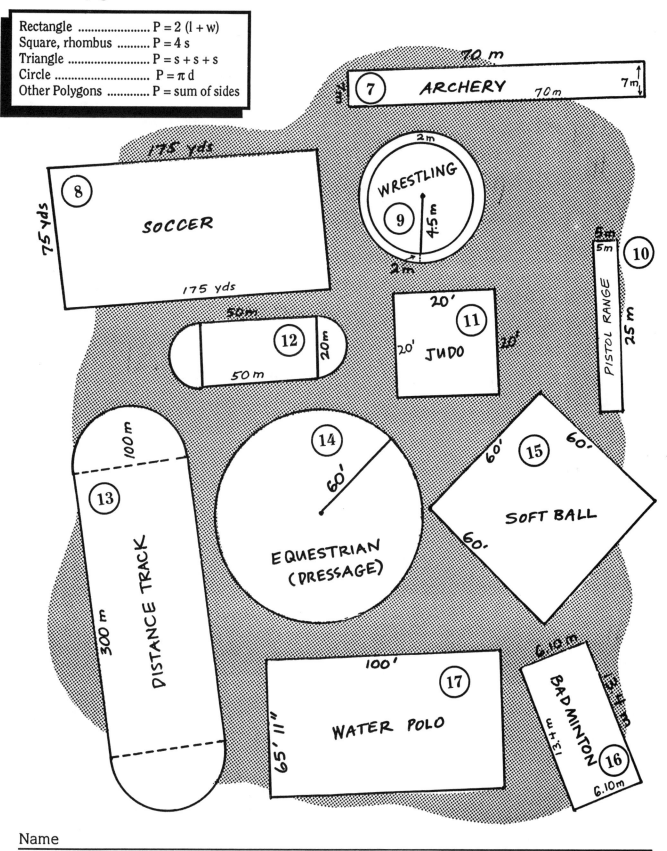

NO HORSING AROUND

When Stephanie trains her horse for dressage, she spends many hours requiring the horse to do precise movements. Use the circle diagram to answer the questions about each command.

1. Stand at the center.
   (What point is this?) _____

2. Walk both diameters.
   (Name the line segments.) _____

3. Walk the radii.
   (Name the segments.) _____

4. Walk an acute central angle.
   (Name the angle.) _____

5. Walk an obtuse central angle.
   (Name the angle.) _____

6. Walk all intersecting chords.
   (Name the chords.) _____

7. Walk 3 chords.
   (Name 3 chords.) _____

8. Walk 5 arcs.
   (Name 5 arcs.) _____

9. Walk all central angles.
   (Name all central angles.) _____

10. The horse walks $\overline{MN}$.
    This is 12 feet. How long is $\overline{MK}$? _____

Read the following statements concerning circles. Determine if each statement is **always** true (A), **sometimes** true (S), or **never** true (N).

_____ 11. Some arcs are line segments.

_____ 12. Chords are diameters.

_____ 13. All radii in a cirle are the same length.

_____ 14. All diameters in a circle are the same length.

_____ 15. A central angle has its vertex on the circle.

_____ 16. Small circles measure less than 360 degrees. Larger circles measure more than 360 degrees.

_____ 17. Circles are congruent.

_____ 18. Circles are regular polygons.

_____ 19. All radii are half the length of all diameters of a particular circle.

_____ 20. All diameters pass through the center of the circle.

Name _____

CIRCULAR REASONING

A circle is a common sight at the Olympic Games, starting with the rings in the Olympic symbol. Many of the sports contain elements that are circular or spherical in shape. Use the formula for circumference ($C = \pi d$) to answer these questions about circles found around the Olympic venues.

1. One of the 5 Olympic Rings on the front of the Olympic Village sign has a diameter of 3 meters. What is the circumference of one of the rings?

2. In mountain biking, an "endo" is a "graceful" maneuver that occurs when a rider is catapulted from the bike as the rear wheel lifts off the ground. This is an easy move if the tire has a diameter of 20 inches. What is the circumference of such a tire?

4. A softball is larger than a baseball. The official size is $12\frac{1}{8}$ inches in diameter. What is the circumference of a softball?

5. The table tennis ball is made of celluloid and is approximately 1.5 inches in diameter. What is the circumference of a table tennis ball?

6. Team handball combines the skills of running, jumping, catching, and throwing. The men's handball is 60 centimeters in circumference. What is its diameter?

7. Tennis balls are made from rubber molded into two cups. The cups are cemented together and covered with wool felt. The tennis ball is approximately 2.5 inches in diameter. What is its circumference?

3. Leon Flameng, the first Olympic cyclist to win gold, circled a 333.33 m cement track 300 times to beat out his competition. What was the diameter of that track?

8. Today's discus is make from wood and metal and has the shape of a flying saucer. The athlete must stand in a throwing circle that has a diameter of 2.5 meters. What is the circumference of the throwing circle?

9. In volleyball, the ball is slightly smaller than a basketball. The ball's circumference is about 27 inches. What is its diameter?

10. In the hammer throw, the throwing circle is 7 feet in diameter. What is the circumference of the throwing circle?

Name

SEEING DOUBLE

Synchronized swimming was added to the Summer Olympic Games in 1984. When watching duet synchronized swimming, you think you are seeing double! Look at the geometric figures below and decide if you are seeing double (or congruent shapes) or just two shapes that are similar!

Congruent polygons are exactly the same. **Similar polygons** have the same shape. Their corresponding angles are congruent and their corresponding sides are proportional.

Place the letters after each correct answer on the corresponding blanks below to discover the only American in 20 years to win all 3 synchronized swimming events at a World Championship.

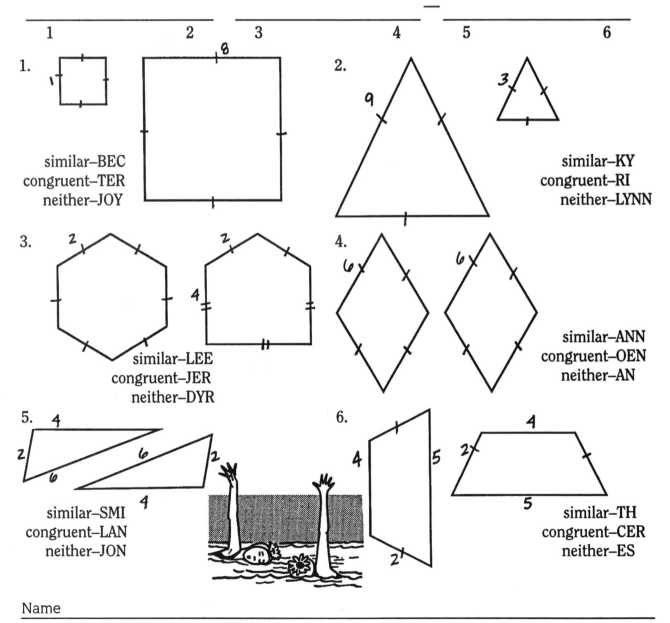

_____ _____ _____   —   _____
  1   2   3   4   5   6

1.

similar–BEC
congruent–TER
neither–JOY

2.

similar–KY
congruent–RI
neither–LYNN

3.

similar–LEE
congruent–JER
neither–DYR

4.

similar–ANN
congruent–OEN
neither–AN

5.

similar–SMI
congruent–LAN
neither–JON

6.

similar–TH
congruent–CER
neither–ES

Name

PLACES AND SPACES

The settings where Olympic athletes compete include places and spaces of all sizes and shapes. Many of them are quadrilaterals (4-sided figures). You can learn something about these spaces by solving the following problems about their areas.

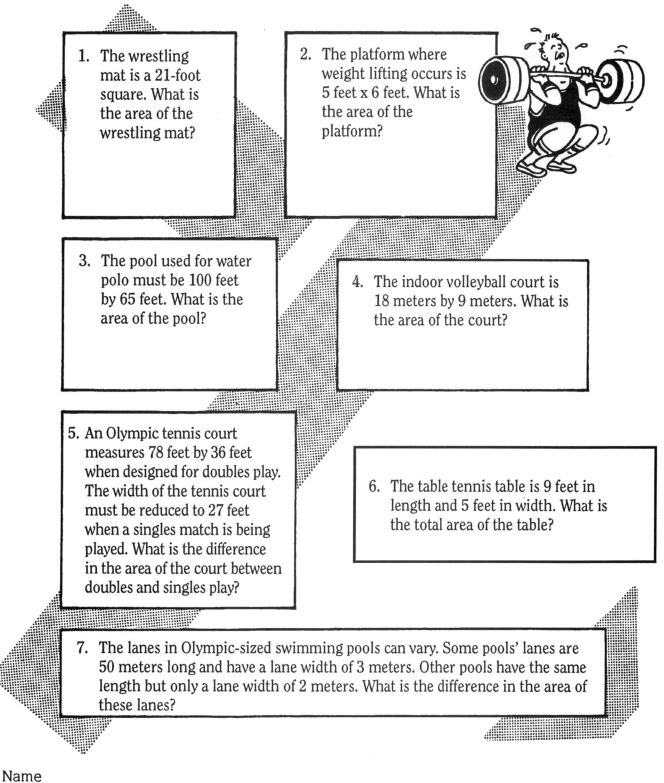

1. The wrestling mat is a 21-foot square. What is the area of the wrestling mat?

2. The platform where weight lifting occurs is 5 feet x 6 feet. What is the area of the platform?

3. The pool used for water polo must be 100 feet by 65 feet. What is the area of the pool?

4. The indoor volleyball court is 18 meters by 9 meters. What is the area of the court?

5. An Olympic tennis court measures 78 feet by 36 feet when designed for doubles play. The width of the tennis court must be reduced to 27 feet when a singles match is being played. What is the difference in the area of the court between doubles and singles play?

6. The table tennis table is 9 feet in length and 5 feet in width. What is the total area of the table?

7. The lanes in Olympic-sized swimming pools can vary. Some pools' lanes are 50 meters long and have a lane width of 3 meters. Other pools have the same length but only a lane width of 2 meters. What is the difference in the area of these lanes?

Name

SMOOTH SAILING

In the early days of yachting, the sails were no more than bedspreads that were attached by clothesline. Now the main type of sail on yachting vessels is triangular. Look at the sails below and determine the area of each.

$A = \frac{1}{2}bh$

1. _____   3. _____   5. _____   7. _____

2. _____   4. _____   6. _____   8. _____

HOMEWORK FROM HOME

Friends back home decided to surprise Eric with some homework from his school. They decided he shouldn't get behind on the math they were doing in class. So they sent him postcards at the Olympic Village. These postcards asked him to find   the area of trapezoids. But, in choosing the correct answer for each problem,   he was also solving a puzzle that sent him a message. Can you figure out the   message his friends sent?

1.
5"
4"
10"

F 200 in²

G 30 in²

A 60 in²

5.
37 m
54.2 m
81 m

B 177,422.4 m²

L 3492.8 m²

F 6985.6 m²

2.
9'
12'
15'

O 144 ft²

D 1,260 ft²

E 288 ft

6.
8"
6"
19"

O 912 in²

R 456 in²

U 81 in²

3.
11 cm
9 cm
4 cm

T 396 cm²

O 67.5 cm²²

P 198 cm²

7.
14½ "
6"
10½ "

C 75 in²

D 913.5 in²

E 456.75 in²

4.
8.4 cm
2.4 cm
7.6 cm

D 19.2 cm²

X 153.2 cm²

W 76.61 cm²

8.
3½ '
2½ '
5½ '

K 11.97 ft²

L 23.94 ft²

M 51.21 ft²

1	2	3	4	5	6	7	8

Name _____

SIZABLE DIFFERENCES

When a group of athletes got together for lunch, they were all wearing T-shirts with pictures of the balls used in their sports. They got into a grand discussion about whether or not the size of the ball made the sport harder or easier. The final consensus was that size had nothing to do with difficulty—all their sports took great skill! But, just to satisfy their curiosity, they measured the pictures on their T-shirts and ranked the areas from largest to smallest.

I. Complete the chart.

Sport	Diameter	Radius	Area
1. soccer ball	d = 8.5 in.		
2. women's softball	d = 3.82 in.		
3. table tennis ball	d = 1.5 in.		
4. men's team handball	d = 2.31 in.		
5. women's team handball	d = 2.23 in.		
6. tennis ball	d = 2.5 in.		
7. basketball	d = 9 in.		
8. volleyball	d = 8 in.		
9. baseball	d = 3 in.		

II. Rank the balls in order from largest to smallest.

1. _____
2. _____
3. _____
4. _____
5. _____
6. _____
7. _____
8. _____
9. _____

Name

ON TARGET

In the sport of archery, archers shoot 72 arrows at the target. A score of 720 is a perfect score. See if you can get a score this high by identifying congruent angles in the figures below and answering questions about the angles. Each correct answer is worth 60 points.

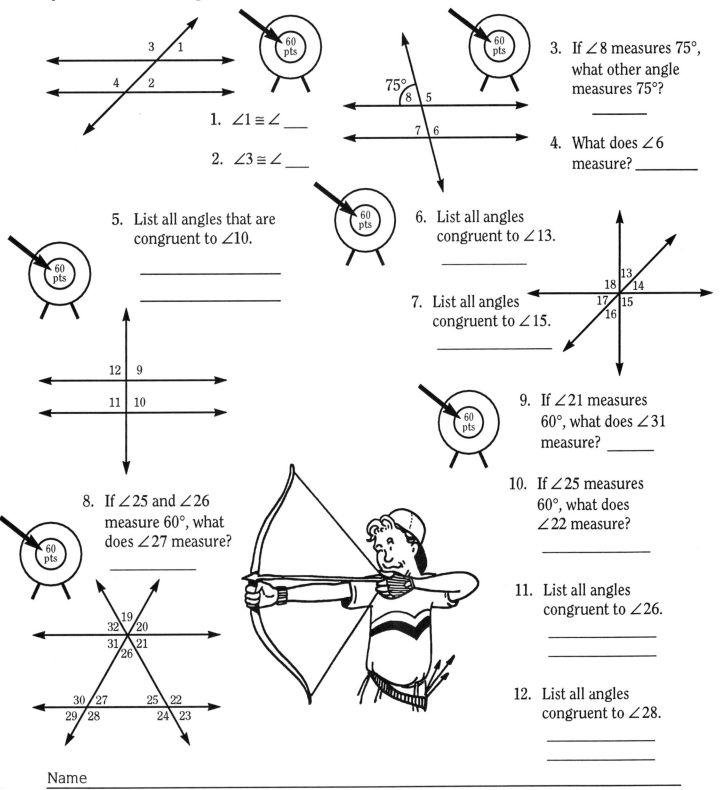

1. ∠1 ≅ ∠ ___

2. ∠3 ≅ ∠ ___

3. If ∠8 measures 75°, what other angle measures 75°?

   _____

4. What does ∠6 measure? _____

5. List all angles that are congruent to ∠10.

   _____

   _____

6. List all angles congruent to ∠13.

   _____

7. List all angles congruent to ∠15.

   _____

8. If ∠25 and ∠26 measure 60°, what does ∠27 measure?

   _____

9. If ∠21 measures 60°, what does ∠31 measure? _____

10. If ∠25 measures 60°, what does ∠22 measure?

    _____

11. List all angles congruent to ∠26.

    _____

    _____

12. List all angles congruent to ∠28.

    _____

    _____

Name _____

FLIPPED FIGURES

Divers and gymnasts do plenty of flips and turns. Geometric figures can be flipped and turned, too. But if the measurements of the sides and angles stay the same, a figure will not change. When a polygon has the same numbers of sides and angles, with the same measurements as another figure, the figures are **congruent**, even if the figures are in a different position.

Match each polygon in Column A with its congruent polygon in Column B.

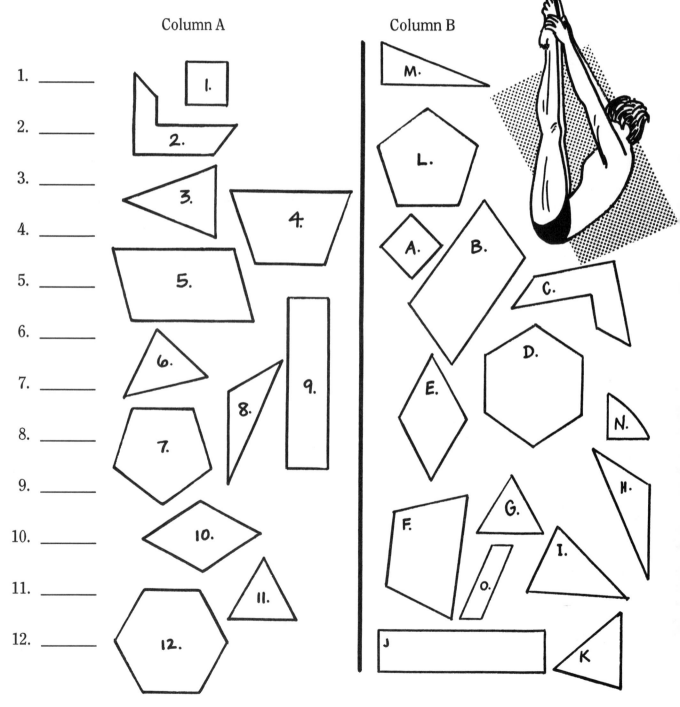

Column A

Column B

1. _____
2. _____
3. _____
4. _____
5. _____
6. _____
7. _____
8. _____
9. _____
10. _____
11. _____
12. _____

Name

DUFFEL BAG MATH

If you snooped inside the duffel bag of this Olympic athlete, you would find some containers that are space figures. Identify each space figure by name, then find its volume. (Round each answer to the nearest hundredth.)

Which container has the greatest volume?

Prism	$V = Bh$
Sphere	$V = \frac{4}{3}\pi r^3$
Cone	$V = \pi r^2 h \frac{1}{3}$
Cylinder	$V = \pi r^2 h$

r = radius
h = height
B = area of base

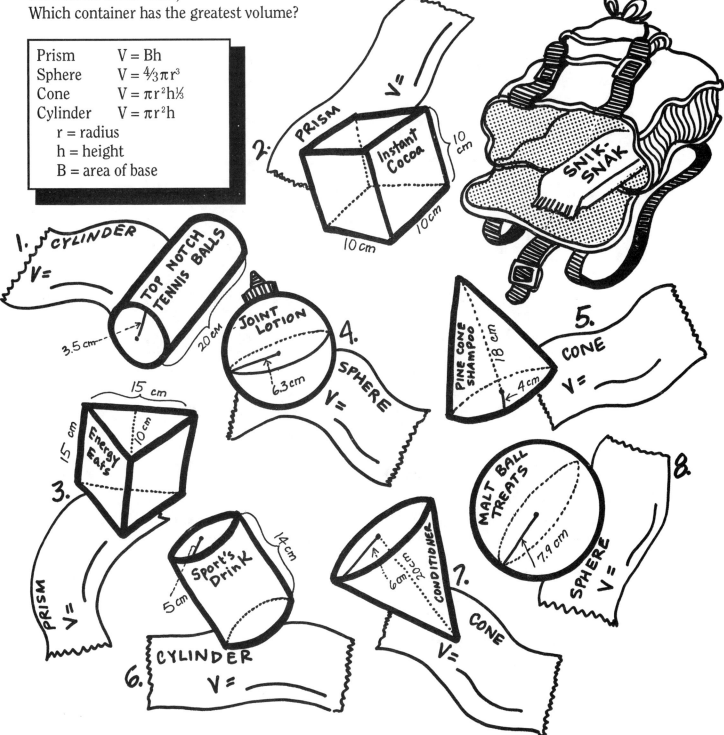

2. PRISM   V=
Instant Cocoa
10 cm
10 cm
10 cm

SNIK-SNAK

1. CYLINDER   V=
TOP NOTCH TENNIS BALLS
3.5 cm
20 cm

4. JOINT LOTION
SPHERE   V=
6.3 cm

5. PINE CONE SHAMPOO
18 cm
4 cm
CONE   V=

3. PRISM   V=
Energy Eats
15 cm
15 cm
10 cm

6. CYLINDER   V=
Sport's Drink
14 cm
5 cm

7. CONDITIONER
20 cm
6 cm
CONE   V=

8. MALT BALL TREATS
7.9 cm
SPHERE   V=

PRISM & PYRAMID CALCULATIONS

One night after the games the athletes from Egypt and Mexico were discussing the unique land-marks in their countries. They quickly realized that both groups had pyramids in their homeland. Read about the pyramids below and determine their volume. Using the formula V= ⅓ Bh, find the volume of each pyramid.

EGYPT

1. The Pyramid at Madydun is 93 m high. The Egyptian athletes weren't sure of the other measurements, so they estimated. They believed that the pyramid had a square base that was about 75 m on each side.
2. The largest pyramid in the world is Khufu. Its square base measures 230 m on each side, and it is 147 m high.

CENTRAL AMERICA

3. The Pyramid of the Sun is the largest pyramid in Mexico. It is 66 m high. The athletes esti-mated that the base of the pyramid was a square that measures about 45 m on each side.

Later, the athletes discussed the difference between a pyramid and a prism. They remembered that the volume formula for a rectangular prism was $V = Bh$ or $V = lwh$.
Match the following rectangular prisms with their volumes.

_____ 4. l = 15 in., w = 13 in., h = 17 in   a. 13.125 in³

_____ 5. l = 2.5 in., w = 1.5 in., h = 3.5 in   b. 3315 in³

_____ 6. l = 1.2 in., w = 1.2 in., h = 1.2 in   c. 1.728 cm³

Use with page 31.

Name

PRISM & PYRAMID CALCULATIONS, CONTINUED

Use with page 30.

Match the following triangular prisms with their volumes. Don't forget how to measure a triangular base! Find the area of the triangular base and then multiply that number by the height of the prism.

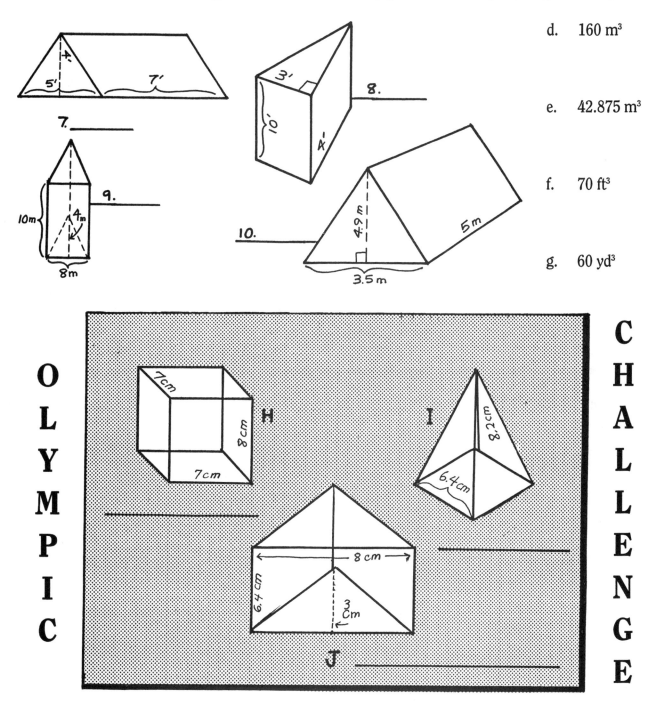

d. 160 m³

e. 42.875 m³

f. 70 ft³

g. 60 yd³

Which has the greatest volume? _____

Name _____

DO YOU SPEAK METRIC?

Most measurements found at the Olympics are metric. This is because the metric system is one that is used and understood all over the world, no matter what the language is. Show how well you understand the different units of metric measurement by answering these questions about Olympic measurements.

1. If in the long jump two opponents were very close, would you measure their jumps in centimeters or meters?

2. To mark off the running track for the relay race, would you measure the track in centimeters or meters?

3. If a thirsty biker were buying a water bottle for his bike, would he want a liter or a kiloliter of water?

4. To set up the distance between the hurdles would you measure in meters or millimeters?

5. Are marathon races usually measured in meters or kilometers?

6. Would it make sense to measure the diameter of a softball in meters of centimeters?

7. Would the weights that weight lifters use be measured in grams or kilograms?

8. Would a tall swimmer give his height in centimeters or kilometers?

9. Would the gold in a gold medal be weighed in grams or decagrams?

10. Would the length of the blade on a fencing sword be measured in millimeters or centimeters?

11. If you needed to know how many soccer balls would fit into a large bag, would you calculate the bag's volume using cubic millimeters or cubic centimeters?

12. Would the amount of water in a diving pool be measured in milliliters or kiloliters?

13. Which unit is more likely to be used to measure the height of a pole vaulter's jump: grams, liters, meters, or kilometers?

14. Is it likely that an athlete could throw the javelin 30 kilometers?

15. Do you think an Olympic basketball player might weigh about 50 grams?

Name

IT TAKES TEAMWORK

Basketball team members must work together very effectively to have a chance of winning. Teamwork can help you solve math problems, too. Here are some measurements showing how far the ball moved forward in different situations. Work with a partner to change these linear metric measurements into different units.

Use this sentence to help you remember the order of size of metric units.

Kids	Have	Done	Metrics	During	Cooperative	Math Lessons
Kilo-	*Hecto-*	*Deka-*	*Meters*	*Deci-*	*Centi-*	*Milli-*
1000	100	10	1	0.1	0.01	0.001

1. 10 m = _____ mm

2. 3.54 m = _____ cm

3. 137 m = _____ km

4. 1 km = _____ cm

5. 12.34 m = _____ cm

6. 10 cm = _____ mm

7. 124.5 km = _____ cm

8. 1.2 mm = _____ cm

9. 45.67 m = _____ mm

10. 0.99 km = _____ m

11. 56.72 m = _____ km

12. 45.67 cm = _____ m

13. 569 mm = _____ m

14. 98.43 cm = _____ m

15. 900 mm = _____ cm

16. 456 mm = _____ m

17. 27 km = _____ cm

18. 876.1 mm = _____ cm

19. 0.851 km = _____ m

20. 567 mm = _____ km

Name _____

THE GREAT MEASUREMENT SWITCH

The metric system is used for measurements at the Olympics. But many U.S. citizens understand their customary system better. How good are you at knowing which metric unit corresponds best to which U.S. measurement unit? Find out by answering these questions with either: inches, feet, yards, miles, pints, quarts, ounces, or pounds.

1. The badminton courts are 13.4 meters.
   The best U.S. customary unit of measure to convert this to would be _____.

2. To score 3 points in Olympic basketball, the player must be 6.25 meters away from the goal.
   The best U.S. customary unit of measure to convert this to would be _____.

3. A flyweight in boxing weighs 51 kg.
   The best U.S. customary unit of measure to convert this to would be _____.

4. In cycling, the course is measured in kilometers.
   The best U.S. customary unit of measure to convert this to would be _____.

5. The men's platform in diving is 10 meters high.
   The best U.S. customary unit of measure to convert this to would be

   _____.

6. In fencing, the foil can be 1100 millimeters in length.
   The best U.S. customary unit of measure to convert this to would be

   _____.

7. In rowing, the course is 2000 meters.
   The best U.S. customary unit of measure to convert this to would be _____.

8. The sprint race in swimming is 50 meters long.
   The U.S. best customary unit of measure to convert this to would be _____.

9. The ball used in table tennis weighs 2.5 grams.
   The best U.S. customary unit of measure to convert this to would be _____.

10. The handball is 60 centimeters in circumference.
    The best U.S. customary unit of measure to convert this to would be _____.

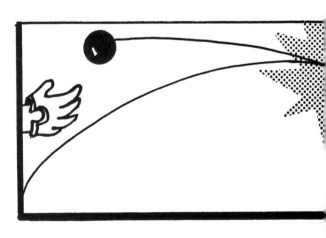

Use with page 35.

Name

THE GREAT MEASUREMENT SWITCH, CONTINUED

Use with page 34.

11. The take-off board in the long jump is 20 centimeters wide.
The best U.S. customary unit of measure to convert this to would be _____ .

12. The discus weighs 2 kilograms.
The best U.S. customary unit of measure to convert this to would be _____ .

13. The men's javelin must weigh at least 800 grams.
The best U.S. customary unit of measure to convert this to would be _____ .

14. The volleyball court measures 18 meters.
The best U.S. customary unit of measure to convert this to would be _____ .

15. Each time a weight lifter makes a lift attempt, the weight lifted must be increased by at least 2.5 kilograms. *The best U.S. customary unit of measure to convert this to would be* _____ .

16. The men's biathalon has a 30-kilometer relay. *The best U.S. customary unit of measure to convert this to would be* _____ .

17. One track and field event for women is a 1500 meter run.
The best U.S. customary unit of measure to convert this to would be _____ .

18. Divers leaving the 10-meter platform can travel up to 48 kilometers per hour into the water.
The best U.S. customary unit of measure to convert this to would be _____ .

19. The smallest gymnast at the 1996 Summer Olympics weighed about 36 kilograms.
The best U.S. customary unit of measure to convert this to would be _____ .

20. A singles tennis court measures 23.8 m x 8.2 m.
The best U.S. customary unit of measure to convert this to would be _____ .

21. A tennis ball weighs less than 500 grams.
The best U.S. customary unit of measure to convert this to would be _____ .

22. The winner of the pole vault at the 1996 Summer Olympics cleared a bar that was over 579 centimeters from the ground.
The best U.S. customary unit of measure to convert this to would be _____ .

23. A runner drank 8 liters of water on one hot day at the Olympics.
The best U.S. customary unit of measure to convert this to would be _____ .

24. Many of the race courses for women kayakers are 500 meters long.
The best U.S. customary unit of measure to convert this to would be _____ .

Name _____

MIXED-UP MEASURES

Sometimes Olympic judges and officials get into some sticky predicaments. The mix-ups here have to do with measurements given in the wrong units. Help them make sense out of the mixed-up measures.

1. Art the Archer hit a bulls-eye from 105 feet. Convert 105 feet to yards. _____

2. The workers were trying to mark off the length of the badminton court. Someone told them it was 528 inches long. How many feet is that? _____

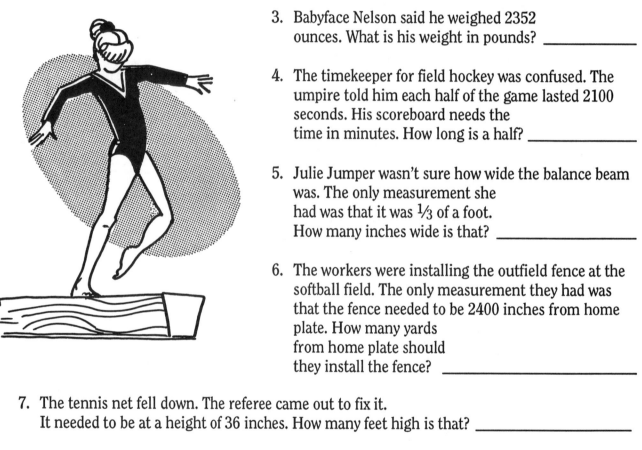

3. Babyface Nelson said he weighed 2352 ounces. What is his weight in pounds? _____

4. The timekeeper for field hockey was confused. The umpire told him each half of the game lasted 2100 seconds. His scoreboard needs the time in minutes. How long is a half? _____

5. Julie Jumper wasn't sure how wide the balance beam was. The only measurement she had was that it was $\frac{1}{3}$ of a foot. How many inches wide is that? _____

6. The workers were installing the outfield fence at the softball field. The only measurement they had was that the fence needed to be 2400 inches from home plate. How many yards from home plate should they install the fence? _____

7. The tennis net fell down. The referee came out to fix it. It needed to be at a height of 36 inches. How many feet high is that? _____

8. Daddy Longlegs once jumped 660 inches in the triple jump. How many feet did Daddy jump? _____

9. The 10K run was completed in 1620 seconds by Speedy Sam. How many minutes is that? _____

10. The hammer used in the hammer throw weighs 256 ounces. How many pounds does it weigh? _____

Name _____

MEASUREMENT MATTERS

Knowing how to measure and knowing what unit to use are critical skills for anyone who is involved in sports. Answer the following questions about measurements by circling the correct measurements.

1. Which unit of measure would be appropriate to use to describe the length of a badminton court? (feet, pounds, or inches)

2. In boxing, the athlete gets a 60 (second or hour) break between rounds.

3. In mountain biking, the course is between 4 and 20 (inches, feet, yards, or miles) long.

4. In the Tantrum race, cyclist are riding at approximately 50 (miles, feet, or yards) per hour.

5. The platform diving board is 33 (feet, inches, or yards) high.

6. In 1968, Marion Coakes won the show jumping silver medal with her pony Stroller. The pony was only 57 (inches, feet, or yards) tall.

7. The foil is the sword of choice in fencing. It may be as long as 43.307 (inches, feet, or yards) in length.

8. In field hockey, it is possible for the ball to travel 100 (miles, inches, or feet) an hour.

9. In gymnastics, the balance beam is only a slim 4 (inches, feet, or yards) wide.

10. A softball weighs about 7 (pounds, ounces, or tons).

11. In softball, the pitcher's mound is 40 (feet, inches, miles) from home plate.

12. In the high jump, Dick Browning somersaulted over a bar set at 7 (feet, inches, or yards).

Name

AN OLYMPIC TRADITION

If you follow these directions carefully, you'll create a drawing of a symbol that has represented the Olympics for hundreds of years. Use the next page for your drawing.

1. Beginning at point A draw an equilateral triangle. Label the triangle ABC. Point B is on the left side of the paper and Point C is on the right side of the paper. Each side of the triangle must measure 4 inches.

2. From Point B draw a straight line (toward the top of the paper) that measures $3\frac{3}{4}$ inches. Label this line segment $\overline{BE}$.

3. Using point E as the vertex of the angle, draw $\angle$ BEF. It must measure 40°. (Point F should be to the right of point E.) The length of $\overline{EF}$ must measure 1 inch.

4. Find the midpoint of $\overline{BC}$ and label it point J. From point J, measure (towards the top of the paper) $5\frac{1}{4}$ inches and draw a point. Label it point G.

5. From point C draw a staight line (toward the top of the paper) that measures $5\frac{1}{2}$ inches. Label this segment $\overline{CI}$.

6. Find the midpoint of $\overline{JC}$. Label this point K.

7. Place point H $4\frac{1}{2}$ inches above point K.

8. Using point F as the vertex of the angle, draw $\angle$ EFG. It must measure 75°. The length of $\overline{FG}$ must measure $2\frac{1}{2}$ inches. Point G is near the top of the paper.

9. Using point H as the vertex, draw $\angle$ GHI. It must measure 80°. The length of $\overline{GH}$ must measure 1 inch and $\overline{HI}$ must measure $1\frac{1}{2}$ inches.

10. What Olympic symbol did you create? _____

Use page 39 for your drawing.

Name

AN OLYMPIC TRADITION, CONTINUED

Use with page 38.

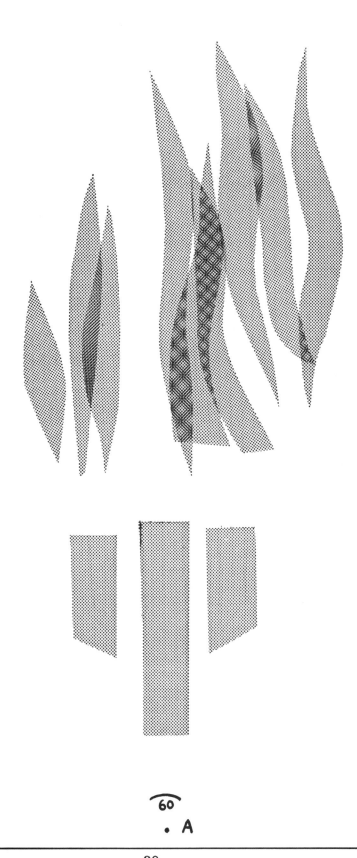

60

• A

WHOSE ROOM IS ROOMIER?

When the U.S. Team arrived at the Olympic Village, they were surprised by their accommodations. Some of the rooms were very large and roomy. Others seemed really small. Below are scale drawings of their rooms. You can compare the sizes of the rooms by doing some measuring. Note the scale: 1 cm = 2 ft. Then measure and find the area and perimeter of each room. *(Note: the rooms are slightly irregular, so your measurements may be approximate.)*

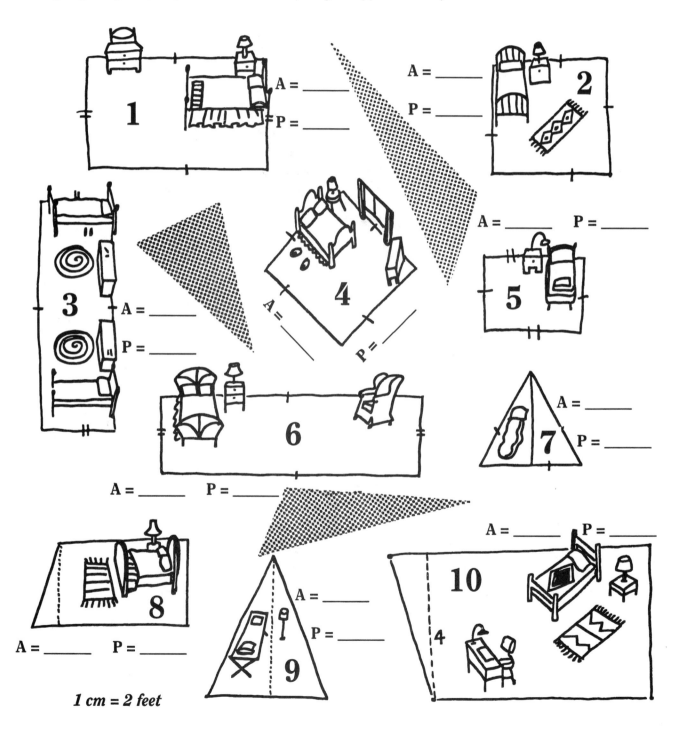

1 cm = 2 feet

Name

EMPIRICAL, SPHERICAL FACTS

The sports in the Summer Olympics use balls of many different kinds. The shape rarely varies—because most balls are spheres. But they differ greatly in size and weight. This chart shows the size and weight of some of the balls you'd expect to find at the Olympics. Use the statistics on the chart to answer the questions. (You'll need to use a dictionary or math glossary to refresh your knowledge about the statistical concepts of **mean, median,** and **range.**)

Type of Ball	Circumference	Weight
Baseball	9.25 inches	5.25 ounces
Basketball	30 inches	22 ounces
Soccer	28 inches	16 ounces
Tennis	8.25 inches	2.062 ounces
Volleyball	26 inches	9.25 ounces
Polo	11 inches	4.5 ounces
Ping-Pong	4.7 inches	0.091 ounces

1. Which type of ball is the closest in circumference to the volleyball? _____

2. Which type of ball is the closest in circumference to the basketball? _____

3. What is the range of the circumferences of the balls? _____

4. What is the mean of the circumferences of the ball? _____

5. What is the median of the circumferences of the balls? _____

6. Which of the balls are the closest in weight? _____

7. Which ball is the heaviest? _____

8. What is the mean weight of the balls in the chart? _____

9. What is the median weight of the balls in the chart? _____

10. What is the range of the weight of the balls in the chart? _____

11. Rank order the balls from lightest to heaviest. _____

Name

MIDNIGHT SNACKS

Some members of the U.S. swim team paid a midnight visit to the vending machines for snacks. They were astounded by the prices! Which snacks should they buy to get the most for their money? If all the snacks below cost the same, figure out which one holds the greatest volume of food. Measure and calculate the volume for each. Measure in centimeters, and note the scale: 1 cm =10 cm. (Note: Figures may be slightly irregular so your answers may be approximate.)

Name

WRESTLING WITH ANGLES

Wrestling matches are won by receiving points for performing certain moves or techniques. One way to score points is called **exposure**. A wrestler gets points for exposure when he turns his opponent's shoulders to the mat. Points are awarded when the opponent's back is less than 90° from the mat. (His back is forming an acute angle with the mat!)

Score your own points by using a protractor to correctly measure these angles.

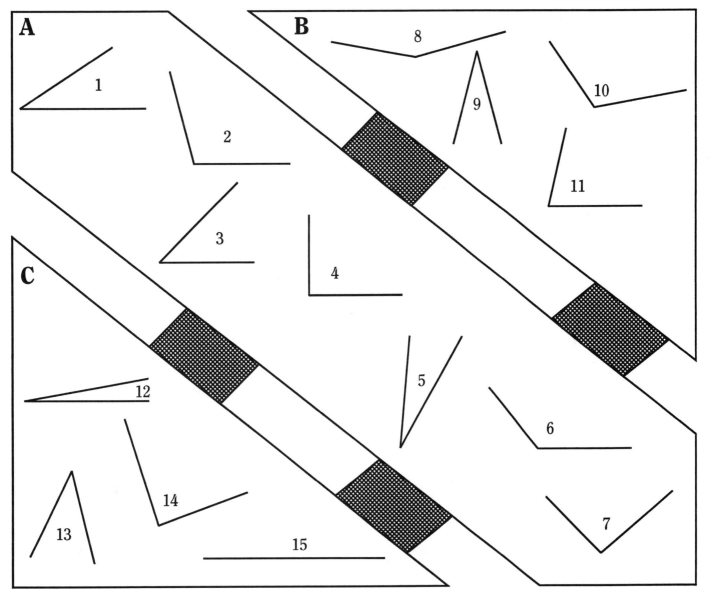

Name _____

ABOUT HOW MUCH?

Hundreds of measurements are needed to plan and run the Olympic Games. Not all of these measurements can be exact; many of them must be estimated. Here are some Olympic problems that need estimates.

1. The Olympics began around 900 BC. Approximately how many years ago did the Olympics begin?
    A. 1000 years ago   B. 2000 years ago   C. 3000 years ago

2. In 1900, 1319 men and 11 women were involved in the games. About how many participants were there?
    A. 1000 athletes   B. 1350 athletes   C. 1400 athletes

3. The TV rights for the 1968 Olympics were sold for $4.5 million. This included 44 hours of broadcasting. Approximately how much per hour did the TV rights cost?
    A. $100,000 per hour   B. $10,000 per hour   C. $1,000,000 per hour

4. In Olympic basketball the three-point shot distance is not the same as the NBA three-point distance. The NBA distance is 22 feet. In the Olympics, it is about 20.5 feet. What is the approximate difference, in inches, of these two measurements?
    A. About 30 inches   B. Around 20 inches   C. 10 inches

5. There are 12 weight classes in boxing at the Olympics. The light featherweight weighs up to 112 pounds and the super heavyweight may weigh up to 201 pounds. About how many pounds separate these two weight classes?
    A. A little over 100 pounds
    B. A little under 100 pounds
    C. About 200 pounds

6. Leon Flameng, the first Olympic cyclist to win gold, circled a 333.33 m track 300 times. Altogether he cycled about
    A. 100,000 meters
    B. 1000 meters
    C. 1,000,000 meters

7. In the equestrian three-day event, a horse is expected to jump a 3'11" obstacle. About how many inches high is this obstacle?
    A. 40 inches
    B. 48 inches
    C. 60 inches

Use with page 45.

Name

ABOUT HOW MUCH?, CONTINUED

Use with page 44.

8. The foil is the sword that the majority of fencers use in the Olympics. It is about 44 inches long. About how many feet long is a foil?

    A. 5 feet
    B. 3 feet
    C. 4 feet

9. If you are a gymnast in college, according to NCAA guidelines you are allowed to practice no more than 20 hours a week. If a college gymnast kept to this training schedule for 4 years, about how many hours would the gymnast practice during his or her college career?

    A. 4000 hours
    B. 2000 hours
    C. 80 hours

10. Judo is performed on a 20 foot–square mat. About how many yards wide is the judo mat?

    A. 8 yards   B. 9 yards   C. 7 yards

11. The softball used in the Olympics is between 11⅞ and 12⅛ inches in diameter. It weighs 6¼ ounces to 7 ounces. If you were telling a friend about the Olympic softball, which statement reflects the best estimate?

    A. The softball is about 12 inches in diameter and weighs about 6 ounces.
    B. The softball is about 12 inches in diameter and weighs about 7 ounces.
    C. The softball is about 7 inches in diameter and weighs about 12 ounces.

12. Carl Lewis's best jump in Barcelona was 8.67 feet. What it the best estimate of this gold medal jump?

    A. 10 feet   B. 8.5 feet   C. 5 feet

13. Mary Decker Slaney was the first woman to run 880 yards in less than 2 minutes. About how many yards is she running a minute?

    A. 400 yards   B. 450 yards   C. 500 yards

14. Imagine that you were planning to spend 5 days at the Olympics. Use the numbers below to determine about how much money you should take with you to the games. (Don't forget to leave a little room in your budget for souvenirs!)

    Motel Room......... *$170.00 a night*   *Event Tickets* .... *$100.00 a day*
    Food .... *$30.00 a day*   *Transportation*......... *$15.95 a day*

    A. About $2000   B. About $500   C. About $4000

Name

WEIGHTY ISSUES

Weight lifting was part of the regimen of classic Greek athletes. They used stones that were held in one hand. These weights were later referred to as dumbbells. In 1928, one-handed weight lifting was abolished. The competition now consists of the "press," the "snatch," and the "jerk." Medals are awarded in each of the following ten different body weight classifications. Convert each of the weight classifications into pounds.

Use the following formula

$$1 \text{ kg} = 2.203 \text{ lb}$$

and then round your answer to the nearest pound.

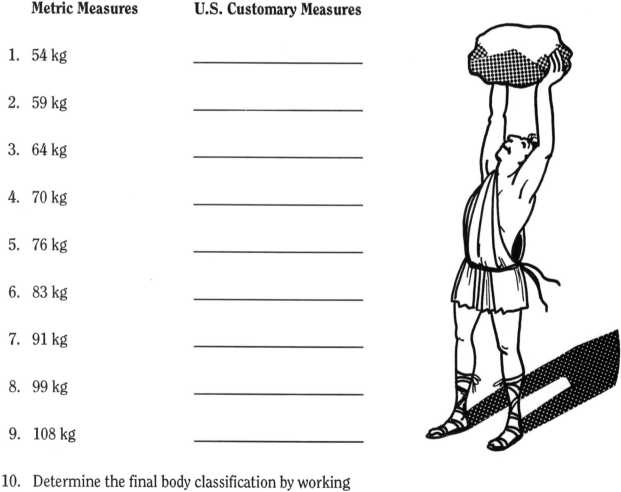

Metric Measures	U.S. Customary Measures
1. 54 kg	_____
2. 59 kg	_____
3. 64 kg	_____
4. 70 kg	_____
5. 76 kg	_____
6. 83 kg	_____
7. 91 kg	_____
8. 99 kg	_____
9. 108 kg	_____

10. Determine the final body classification by working backwards. The International Olympic Committee has imposed a 250-pound limit. Approximately how many kilograms would be the most an athlete in this event could weigh? _____

Name _____

THE HEAT IS ON

At the 1996 Summer Olympics in Atlanta, Georgia, one of the greatest concerns was the heat. Officials kept a close watch on the temperatures. Athletes had to drink plenty of fluids to avoid dehydration.

Record the temperature shown on each thermometer below.

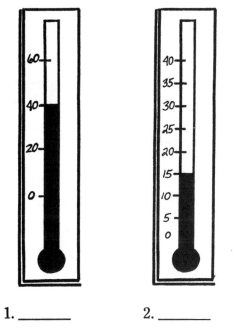

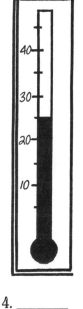

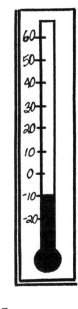

1. _____   2. _____   3. _____   4. _____   5. _____

Use a red pencil or marker to indicate on each thermometer the temperature written below it.

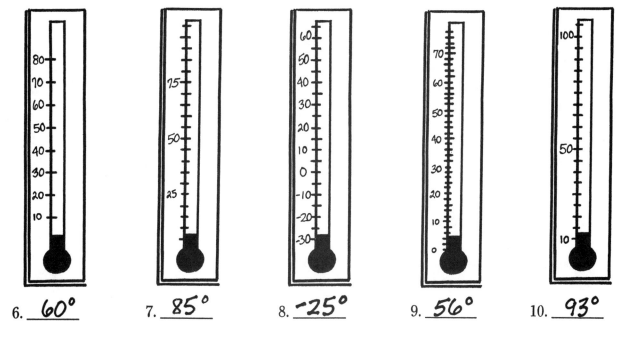

6. _**60°**_   7. _**85°**_   8. _**-25°**_   9. _**56°**_   10. _**93°**_

Name _____

TIME FLIES, AND SO DOES MICHAEL JOHNSON!

Michael Johnson is the only person ever to have run the 400 meter race in less than 44 seconds and the 200 meter distance in less than 20 seconds.

1. Using the formula
$r \times t = d$,
determine how
fast Michael
Johnson ran the
400 meter race.

_____

meters per second

2. Using the formula
$r \times t = d$,
determine how
fast Michael
Johnson ran the
200 meter race.

_____

meters per second

Bob Kennedy carried the United States hopes for the gold in the 1996 Summer Olympic games. His personal records include running the 5,000 meter race in a little over 13 minutes and the 3000 meter race in about 8 minutes.

3. Using the formula $r \times t = d$, determine how fast Bob Kennedy ran the 5000 meter race.

_____ meters per minute

4. Using the formula $r \times t = d$, determine how fast Bob Kennedy ran the 3000 meter race.

_____ meters per minute

5. Gail Devers has won gold medals in the Olympics and in the World Championships. In the space below, draw a $2\frac{1}{2}$ inch line. That's how much distance separated Gail from runner-up Juliet Cuthbert in the 1992 games.

6. Mary Decker Slaney is a middle distance running legend. She was the first woman to run 880 yards in less than 2 minutes. Use the formula $r \times t = d$ to determine how fast Mary Slaney was running.

_____ yards per minute

7. Compare Michael Johnson's speed with
Bob Kennedy's speed. Who is faster? _____

Name

APPENDIX

CONTENTS

GLOSSARY OF GEOMETRY
AND MEASUREMENT TERMS

ALTITUDE OF A TRIANGLE—The distance between a point on the base and the vertex of the opposite angle, measured along a line which is perpendicular to the base. (The altitude is also referred to as the height of the triangle.)

ADJACENT ANGLE—Angles that have the same vertex and a common side between them.

ADJACENT SIDE—The leg next to the given angle in a right triangle.

ANGLE—A figure formed by two rays having a common endpoint (vertex).

    ACUTE ANGLE—An angle which measures less than 90°.

    RIGHT ANGLE—An angle which measures 90°.

    OBTUSE ANGLE—An angle which measures more than 90° and less than 180°.

    STRAIGHT ANGLE—An angle which measures 180°.

    CENTRAL ANGLE—An angle formed by two radii of a circle.

    COMPLEMENTARY ANGLES—Two angles whose measures added together equal 90°.

    CONGRUENT ANGLES—Angles that have the same measure.

    CORRESPONDING ANGLES—Angles formed when a line intersects two parallel lines. Corresponding angles are congruent.

    SUPPLEMENTARY ANGLES—Two angles whose measures added together equal 180°.

    VERTICAL ANGLES—Angles formed opposite one another when two lines intersect. Vertical angles are congruent.

ARC—A portion of the edge of a circle between any two points on the circle.

AREA—The measure of the region inside a closed plane figure. Area is measured in square units.

AXIS—A number line which may be vertical or horizontal.

AXES—Two perpendicular number lines with a common origin.

BASE— A side of a geometric figure.

BISECT—To divide into two congruent parts.

BISECTOR—A line or ray that divides a segment or angle into two congruent parts.

CAPACITY—The measure of the amount that a container will hold.

CHORD—A line segment having endpoints on a circle.

CIRCLE—A closed curve in which all points on the edge are equidistant from a given point in the same plane.

CIRCUMFERENCE—The distance around a circle. Circumference = π x diameter.

CLOSED FIGURE—A set of points that encloses a region in the same plane; a curve that begins and ends at the same point.

COLLINEAR—2 points are collinear when they are on the same line.

COMPASS—A tool for drawing circles.

CONE—A space figure with a circular base.

CONGRUENT—Of equal size.

COPLANAR—When lines or points are on the same plane, they are coplanar.

CUBE—A space figure having six congruent square faces.

CURVE—A set of points connected by a line segment.

CUSTOMARY UNITS—Units of the measurement system used often in the United States (for instance, inches, feet, pounds, ounces, miles).

CYLINDER—A space figure having two congruent circular bases.

DECAGON—A 10-sided polygon.

DEGREE—
   1. A unit of measure used in measuring angles. A circle contains 360°.
   2. A unit for measuring temperature.

DIAGONAL—A line segment joining two nonadjacent vertices in a polygon.

DIAMETER—A line segment which has its endpoints on the circle and which passes through the center of the circle.

DODECAGON—A polygon with 12 faces.

EDGE—A line segment formed by the intersection of two faces of a geometric space figure.

EQUILATERAL—Having sides of the same length.

FACE—A plane region serving as a side of a space figure.

GEOMETRY—The study of space and figures in space.

GRAM—A standard unit for measuring weight in the metric system.

HEMISPHERE—Half a sphere.

HEPTAGON—A 7-sided polygon.

HEXAGON—A 6-sided polygon.

HYPOTENUSE—The longest side of a right triangle located opposite the right angle.

ICOSAHEDRON—A space figure with 20 faces.

INTERSECTION OF LINES—The point at which two lines meet.

INTERSECTION OF PLANES—A line formed by the set of points at which two planes meet.

LEGS—Sides adjacent to the right angle in a right triangle.

LINE—A set of points along a path in a plane.

LINE SEGMENT—Part of a line consisting of a path between two endpoints.

LINEAR MEASURE (or length)—The measure of distance between two points along a line.

LITER—A metric system unit of measurement for liquid capacity.

MEASUREMENT—The process of finding the length, area, capacity, mass, weight, or amount of something.

MEDIAN OF A TRAPEZOID—The line segment joining the midpoints of the nonparallel sides of a trapezoid.

METER—A metric system unit of linear measurement.

METRIC SYSTEM—A system of measurement based on the decimal system.

MIDPOINT—A point that divides a line segment into two congruent segments.

NONAGON—A nine-sided polygon.

OCTAGON—An eight-sided polygon.

OCTAHEDRON—A space figure with eight faces.

PARALLEL LINES—Lines in the same plane which do not intersect.

PARALLELOGRAM—A quadrilateral whose opposite sides are parallel.

PENTAGON—A five sided polygon.

PERIMETER—The distance around the outside of a closed figure.

PERPENDICULAR LINES—Two lines in the same plane that intersect at right angles.

Pi (π)—The ratio of a circle's circumference to its diameter.
3.141592 . . . (a nonterminating decimal)

PLANE—The set of all points on a flat surface which extends indefinitely in all directions.

PLANE FIGURE—A set of points in the same plane enclosing a region.

POINT—An exact location in space.

POLYGON—A simple closed plane figure having line segments as sides.

POLYHEDRON—A space figure formed by intersecting plane surfaces called faces.

PRISM—A space figure with two parallel congruent polygonal faces (called bases).
The prism is named by the shape of its bases. A triangular prism has a triangle for a base.
A rectangular prism has a rectangle for a base.

PROTRACTOR—An instrument used for measuring angles.

PYRAMID—A space figure having one polygonal base and triangular faces which have a common vertex.

PYTHAGOREAN THEOREM—A proposition stating that, in a right triangle, the sum of the squares of the two shorter sides is equal to the square of the third side.

QUADRILATERAL—A four-sided polygon.

RADIUS—A line segment having one endpoint in the center of a circle and the other on the circle.

RAY—A portion of a line extending from one endpoint indefinitely in one direction.

RECTANGLE—A parallelogram having four right angles.

RHOMBUS—A parallelogram having congruent sides.

SEGMENT—Two points and all points between them.

SIMILARITY—A property of geometric figures having angles of the same size.

SIMPLE CLOSED CURVE OR FIGURE—A closed curve whose path does not intersect itself.

SKEW LINES—Lines that are not in the same plane and do not intersect.

SPACE FIGURE—A figure which consists of a set of points lying in two or more planes.

SPHERE—A space figure formed by a set of points lying equidistant from a center point.

SQUARE—A rectangle with all sides congruent.

SURFACE—A region lying on one plane.

SURFACE AREA—The space covered by a plane region or by the faces of a space figure.

SYMMETRIC FIGURE—A figure having two halves that are reflections of one another. A line of symmetry divides the figure into two congruent parts.

TANGENT—A line which touches a figure at one point and has all its other points outside the figure.

TETRAHEDRON—A space figure with four triangular faces.

TRANSVERSAL—A line that cuts two or more parallel lines.

TRAPEZOID—A quadrilateral having only two parallel sides.

TRIANGLE—A three-sided polygon.

> **ACUTE TRIANGLE**—A triangle in which all three angles are less than 90°.

> **ISOSCELES TRIANGLE**—A triangle with at least two congruent sides.

> **OBTUSE TRIANGLE**—A triangle having one angle greater than 90°.

> **RIGHT TRIANGLE**—A triangle having one 90° angle.

> **SCALENE TRIANGLE**—A triangle in which no two sides are congruent.

VERTEX—A common endpoint of two rays forming an angle, two line segments forming sides of a polygon, or two planes forming a polyhedron.

VERTICAL—A line that is perpendicular to a horizontal base line.

VOLUME—The measure of capacity or space enclosed by a space figure.

54

TABLE OF MEASUREMENTS

METRIC SYSTEM		CUSTOMARY SYSTEM
	LENGTH	
1 centimeter (cm) = 10 millimeters (mm) 1 decimeter (dm) = 10 centimeters (cm) 1 meter (m) = 10 decimeters (dm) 1 meter (m) = 100 centimeters (cm) 1 meter (m) = 1000 millimeters (mm) 1 decameter (dkm) = 10 meters (m) 1 hectometer (hm) = 100 meters (m) 1 kilometer (km) = 100 decameters (dkm) 1 kilometer (km) = 1000 meters (m)		1 foot (ft) = 12 inches (in) 1 yard (yd) = 36 inches (in) 1 yard (yd) = 3 feet (ft) 1 mile (mi) = 5280 feet (ft) 1 mile (mi) = 1760 yards (yd)
	AREA	
1 sq meter (m^2) = 100 sq decimeters (dm^2) 1 sq meter(m^2) = 10,000 sq centimeters (cm^2) 1 hectare (ha) = 0.01 sq kilometer (km^2) 1 hectare(ha) = 10,000 sq meters (m^2) 1 sq kilometer (km^2) = 1,000,000 sq meters (m^2) 1 sq kilometer (km^2) = 100 hectares (ha)		1 sq foot (ft^2) = 144 sq inches (in^2) 1 sq yard (yd^2) = 9 sq feet (ft^2) 1 sq yard (yd^2) = 1296 sq inches (in^2) 1 acre (a) = 4840 sq yards (yd^2) 1 acre (a) = 43,560 sq feet (ft^2) 1 sq mile (mi^2) = 640 acres (a)
	VOLUME	
1 cu decimeter (dm^3) = 0.001 cu meter (m^3) 1 cu decimeter (dm^3) = 1000 cu centimeters (cm^3) 1 cu decimeter (dm^3) = 1 liter (L) 1 cu meter (m^3) = 1,000,000 cu centimeters (cm^3) 1 cu meter (m^3) = 1000 cu decimeters (dm^3)		1 cu foot (ft^3) = 1728 cu inches (in^3) 1 cu yard (yd^3) = 27 cu feet (cu^3) 1 cu yard (yd^3) = 46,656 cu inches (in^3)
	CAPACITY	
1 teaspoon = 5 milliliters (mL) 1 tablespoon = 12.5 milliliters (mL) 1 liter (L) = 1000 milliliters (mL) 1 liter (L) = 1000 cu centimeters (cm^3) 1 liter (L) = 1 cu decimeter (dm^3) 1 liter (L) = 4 metric cups 1 kiloliter (kL) = 1000 liters (L)		1 tablespoon (T) = 3 teaspoons (t) 1 cup (c) = 16 tablespoons (T) 1 cup (c) = 8 fluid ounces (fl oz) 1 pint (pt) = 2 cups (c) 1 pint (pt) = 16 fluid ounces (fl oz) 1 quart (qt) = 4 cups (c) 1 quart (qt) = 2 pints (pt) 1 quart (qt) = 32 fluid ounces (fl oz) 1 gallon (gal) = 16 cups (c) 1 gallon (gal) = 8 pint (pt) 1 gallon (gal) = 4 quarts (qt) 1 gallon (gal) = 128 fluid ounces (fl oz)
	WEIGHT	
1 gram = 1000 milligrams (mg) 1 kilogram (kg) = 1000 grams (g) 1 metric ton (t) = 1000 kilograms (kg)		1 pound (lb) = 16 ounces (oz) 1 ton (T) = 2000 pounds (lb)
	TIME	
1 minute (min) = 60 seconds (sec) 1 hour (hr) = 60 minutes (min) 1 day = 24 hours (hr) 1 week = 7 days		1 year (yr) = 52 weeks 1 year (yr) = 365-366 days 1 decade = 10 years 1 century = 100 years

FORMULAS

Perimeter

Triangle .... $P = a + b + c$
Rectangle .... $P = 2(h + w)$
Circle (circumference) .... $C = 2\pi r^2$

Area

Circle .... $A = \pi r^2$
Square .... $A = s^2$
Triangle .... $A = \frac{1}{2}bh$
Trapezoid .... $A = \frac{1}{2}(b_1 + b_2)h$

Volume

Rectangular or Triangular Prism .... $V = Bh$
(B = area of base)

Pyramid .... $V = \frac{1}{3}Bh$

Cube .... $V = s^3$

Cylinder .... $V = \pi r^2 h$

Cone .... $V = \frac{1}{3}\pi r^2 h$

Sphere .... $V = \frac{4}{3}\pi r^3$

MEASUREMENT CONVERSIONS

From Customary Units to Metric

inch .... 2.54 centimeters
foot .... 30.48 centimeters
yard .... 91 meters
mile .... 1.6 meters
square inch .... 6.45 square centimeters
square foot .... .093 square meters
square yard .... 84 square meters
square mile .... 2.59 square kilometers
acre .... 4047 square meters
cubic inch .... 16.39 cubic centimeters

cubic foot .... 028 square meters
cubic yard .... 76 cubic meters
ounce .... 28.35 grams
pound .... 454 grams
ton .... 907.18 kilograms
pint .... 47 liters
quart .... 95 liters
gallon .... 3.79 liters
bushel .... 35.24 liters

From Metric to Customary

To change centimeters .... to inches .... multiply by .3937
To change meters .... to feet .... multiply by 3.2808
To change kilometers .... to miles .... multiply by .6214
To change liters .... to quarts .... multiply by 1.0567
To change kilograms .... to pounds .... multiply by 2.2046
To change metric tons .... to tons .... multiply by 1.1023

Basic Skills/Geometry & Measurement 6-8+   Copyright ©1997 by Incentive Publications, Inc., Nashville, TN.

GEOMETRY & MEASUREMENT
SKILLS TEST

Each question is worth 1 point.

Use this figure for questions 1-10.

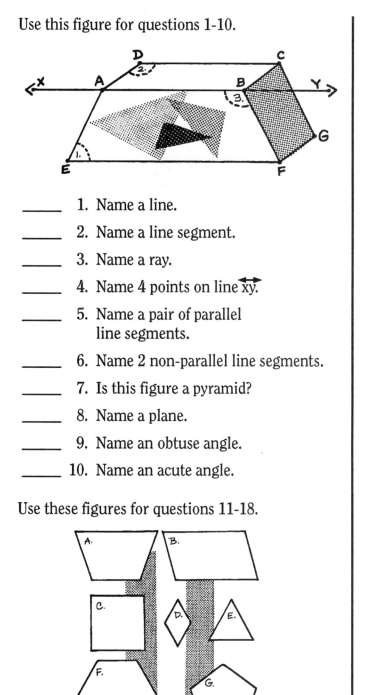

_____ 1. Name a line.

_____ 2. Name a line segment.

_____ 3. Name a ray.

_____ 4. Name 4 points on line $\overleftrightarrow{xy}$.

_____ 5. Name a pair of parallel
line segments.

_____ 6. Name 2 non-parallel line segments.

_____ 7. Is this figure a pyramid?

_____ 8. Name a plane.

_____ 9. Name an obtuse angle.

_____ 10. Name an acute angle.

Use these figures for questions 11-18.

_____ 11. Name 2 rectangles.

_____ 12. Name a square.

_____ 13. Name 2 rhombuses.

_____ 14. Name 2 parallelograms.

_____ 15. Name a pentagon.

_____ 16. Name a hexagon.

_____ 17. Name a trapezoid.

_____ 18. Name a triangle.

Use these figures for questions 19-22.

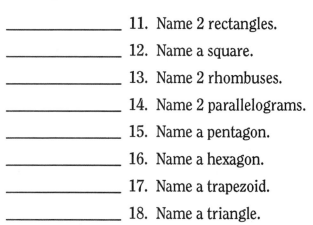

19. Which are scalene triangles? _____

20. Which are isosceles triangles? _____

21. Which are equilateral triangles? _____

22. Which are right triangles? _____

Use this figure for questions 23-27.

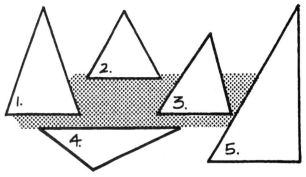

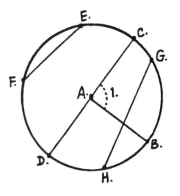

_____ 23. Name 2 chords.

_____ 24. Name a diameter chord.

_____ 25. Name a radius.

_____ 26. Are there any intersecting chords?

_____ 27. Is angle 1 a central angle?

Give the perimeter (or circumference) of each of the figures below.

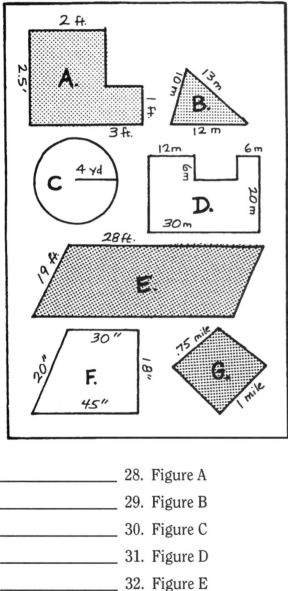

_____ 28. Figure A

_____ 29. Figure B

_____ 30. Figure C

_____ 31. Figure D

_____ 32. Figure E

_____ 33. Figure F

_____ 34. Figure G

Use these figures for questions 35-39.

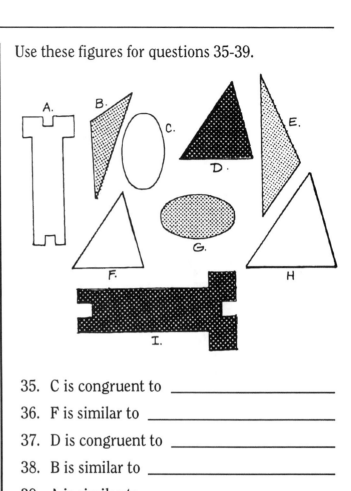

35. C is congruent to _____

36. F is similar to _____

37. D is congruent to _____

38. B is similar to _____

39. A is similar to _____

Find the area of each figure below.

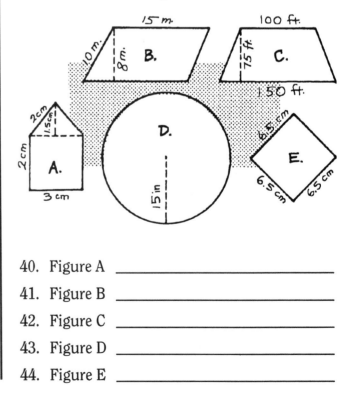

40. Figure A _____

41. Figure B _____

42. Figure C _____

43. Figure D _____

44. Figure E _____

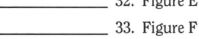
Name _____

Use this figure for questions 45-52.

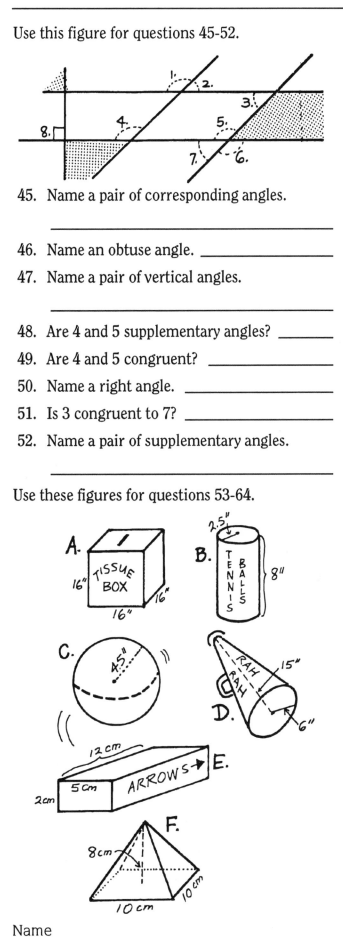

45. Name a pair of corresponding angles.

_____

46. Name an obtuse angle. _____

47. Name a pair of vertical angles.

_____

48. Are 4 and 5 supplementary angles? _____

49. Are 4 and 5 congruent? _____

50. Name a right angle. _____

51. Is 3 congruent to 7? _____

52. Name a pair of supplementary angles.

_____

Use these figures for questions 53-64.

53. Name figure A. _____

54. Give the volume of figure A. _____

55. Name figure B. _____

56. Give the volume of figure B. _____

57. Name figure C. _____

58. Give the volume of figure C. _____

59. Name figure D. _____

60. Give the volume of figure D. _____

61. Name figure E. _____

62. Give the volume of figure E. _____

63. Name Figure F. _____

64. Give the volume of figure F. _____

Use centimeters to measure figures S, T, X, and Y

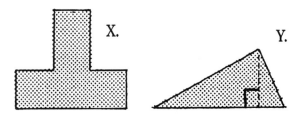

65. Give the perimeter of figure X. _____

66. Give the perimeter of figure Y. _____

67. Give the area of figure X. _____

68. Give the area of figure Y. _____

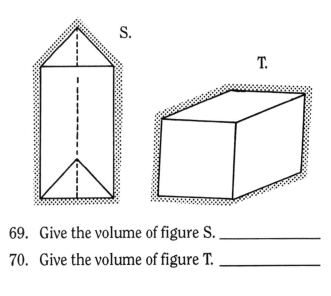

69. Give the volume of figure S. _____

70. Give the volume of figure T. _____

Name _____

Tell what each of these definitions describes.

71. An angle less than 90° _____

72. An angle greater than 90° _____

73. A triangle with 3 equal sides _____

74. A triangle with no equal sides _____

75. A triangle with 2 equal sides _____

Choose the correct answer for each question.

____ 76. 2 lines that intersect each other at right angles are
   a. parallel   b. perpendicular   c. line segments   d. planes

____ 77. 2 angles whose combined measures equal 90° are
   a. right angles   b. congruent angles   c. vertical angles   d. complementary angles

____ 78. 2 angles whose combined measures equal 180° are
   a. supplementary angles b. vertical angles   c. obtuse angles   d. complementary angles

____ 79. a quadrilateral with all angles (but not necessarily all sides) congruent is called a
   a. trapezoid   b. rhombus   c. rectangle   d. parallelogram

____ 80. The area of a trapezoid with bases 4 feet and 5 feet and a height of 6.5 feet is
   a. 130 ft^2 b. 15.5 ft^2 c. 29.25 ft^2 d. 16.25 ft^2

____ 81. The circumference of a circle with a radius of 9 inches is
   a. 28.26 in^2 b. 56.52 in^2 c. 254.34 in^2 d. 1017.36 in^2

____ 82. The volume of a cube with a side of 1.5 meters is
   a. 3.38 m^3 b. 2.25 m^3 c. 121.5 m^3 d. 6 m^3

____ 83. The best metric measure to convert gallons of milk into would be
   a. pints   b. milliliters   c. grams   d. liters

____ 84. The best unit for measuring the depth of a swimming pool would be
   a. centimeters   b. meters   c. kilometers   d. liters

____ 85. The volume of a pyramid with a square base (each side 12 cm) and a height of 8 cm is
   a. 384 cm^3 b. 1152 cm^3 c. 144 cm^3 d. 576 cm^3

____ 86. Which would be the best metric unit for measuring the weight of a soccer ball?
   a. kilograms   b. liters   c. square centimeters d. grams

____ 87. Which metric unit would be best for finding the amount of water in an Olympic diving pool?
   a. square meters   b. quarts   c. liters   d. metric tons

____ 88. 10,000 centimeters would convert to
   a. 10 meters   b. 100 meters   c. 1000 meters   d. .1 meters

____ 89. 4 gallons would convert to
   a. 8 quarts   b. 256 fluid ounces   c. 32 cups   d. 32 pints

____ 90. An athlete who has run a 3000 meter run in 47 races has run approximately
   a. 14 kilometers   b. 1,410 kilometers   c. 141 kilometers   d. 14,100 kilometers

91. A line segment having
   endpoints on a circle is a _____ .

92. 120 lbs is about _____ kg.

93. A 10-sided figure is a _____ .

94. A 19-ft pole vault is _____ meters.

95. A four-sided polygon is a _____ .

96. 24 quarts = _____ gallons

97. 1.75 meters = _____ millimeters

98. 1700 milliliters = _____ liters

99. 48 feet is about _____ meters

100. Volume of a sphere
   with a radius of 7 cm is _____ .

SCORE: Total Points _____ out of a possible 100 points

Name _____

GEOMETRY & MEASUREMENT
SKILLS TEST ANSWER KEY

Questions are worth 1 point each.

1. $\overleftrightarrow{XY}$
2. any of these answers: $\overline{AB}$, $\overline{AE}$, $\overline{AD}$, $\overline{BC}$, $\overline{BF}$, $\overline{CG}$, $\overline{FG}$, $\overline{EF}$, $\overline{DC}$
3. $\overrightarrow{AX}$, $\overrightarrow{BY}$, $\overrightarrow{BX}$, $\overrightarrow{AY}$
4. X, A, B, Y
5. $\overline{EF}$ & $\overline{AB}$, $\overline{AB}$ & $\overline{CD}$, $\overline{AD}$ & $\overline{BC}$, $\overline{BF}$ & $\overline{CG}$, or $\overline{BC}$ & $\overline{FG}$
6. numerous combinations
7. no
8. ABFE or ABCD or BCGF
9. 2
10. 1
11. C, H
12. C
13. C, D
14. B, D
15. G
16. F
17. A
18. E
19. 3, 4, 5
20. 1
21. 2
22. 5
23. Any 2 of these: $\overline{EF}$, $\overline{CD}$, $\overline{GH}$
24. CD
25. AB
26. no
27. yes
28. 8.5
29. 35 m
30. 25.12 yd
31. 112 m
32. 94 ft

33. 113 in
34. 4 mi
35. G
36. H
37. F
38. E
39. I
40. 8.25 cm²
41. 120 ft²
42. 9375 ft²
43. 706.5 in²
44. 42.25 cm²
45. 3 & 7, 4 & 5, 4 & 1
46. 1, 4, 5, or 6
47. 5 & 6
48. no
49. yes
50. 8
51. yes
52. 1 & 2 or 6 & 7
53. cube
54. 4096 m³
55. cylinder
56. 157 in³
57. sphere
58. 381.5 in³
59. cone
60. 565.2 in³
61. prism
62. 120 cm³
63. pyramid
64. 266.67 m³
65. 11 cm
66. 8 cm

67. 4.5 cm²
68. 2.625 cm²
69. 3.5 cm³
70. 8 cm³
71. acute
72. obtuse
73. equilateral
74. scalene
75. isosceles
76. b
77. d
78. a
79. c
80. c
81. b
82. a
83. d
84. b
85. a
86. d
87. c
88. b
89. d
90. c
91. chord
92. 54.48 kg
93. decagon
94. 5.79 m
95. quadrilateral
96. 6
97. 1750
98. 1.7
99. 16
100. 1436.03 cm³

Basic Skills/Geometry & Measurement 6-8+

ANSWERS

p. 10

Answers will vary somewhat, as there are many choices for each.
1. Points: A, B, C, D, E, F, G, H, I, J, K, L, M, N, O
2. $\overleftrightarrow{NI}$ and $\overleftrightarrow{OJ}$
3-6. There are several correct answers for each of these.
7. Planes: ABFG, ABCD, CDHE, GFEH, BCEF, GADH

p. 11

1. acute
2. acute
3. obtuse
4. obtuse
5. obtuse
6. obtuse
7. right
8. obtuse
9. acute
10. acute
11. acute
12. supplementary, 107
13. complementary, 47
14. supplementary, 152
15. complementary, 69

p. 16

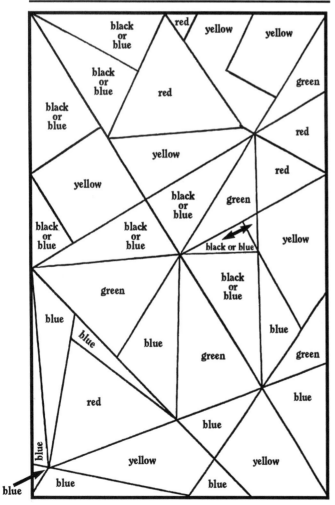

pp. 12-13

1. Information Desk
2. Laundry Building
3. Annex
4. Answers will vary.
5. Medical Center
6. Market
7. True
8. False
9. True
10. Answers will vary.

pp. 14-15

1. Sudan
2. Sweden
3. Kuwait
4. United Kingdom
5. Jamaica
6. Taiwan
7. South Africa
8. Tanzania
9–10. Student designs will vary.

p. 17

A. 1. E
    2. B
    3. C
    4. D
    5. A

B. Check student drawings for accuracy.

pp. 18-19

1. 635.5 m
2. 54 m
3. 84 ft
4. 140 ft
5. 200 m
6. 393 ft
7. 154 m
8. 500 yds
9. 40.82 m
10. 60 m
11. 80 ft
12. 162.8 m
13. 914 m
14. 376.8 ft
15. 240 ft
16. 39 m
17. 331 ft, 10 in

p. 20

1. Point N
2. $\overline{TQ}$ and $\overline{MK}$
3. NT, NK, NQ, NM
4. $\angle$ MNH or $\angle$ HNT
5. $\angle$ HNK
6. $\overline{MK}$ and $\overline{TQ}$, $\overline{MK}$ and $\overline{JQ}$
7. $\overline{TQ}$, $\overline{JQ}$, $\overline{MK}$
8. $\overline{MH}$, $\overline{HT}$, $\overline{TJ}$, $\overline{JK}$, $\overline{KQ}$, $\overline{QM}$
9. $\angle$ MNH, $\angle$ MNT, $\angle$ TNK, $\angle$ MNQ, $\angle$ QNK, $\angle$ HNT
10. 24 feet
11. N
12. S
13. A
14. A
15. N
16. N
17. S
18. N
19. A
20. A

p. 21

1. 9.42 m
2. 62.8 in
3. 106.156 m
4. 38.07 in
5. 4.71 in
6. 19.108 cm
7. 7.85 in
8. 7.85 m
9. 8.59 in
10. 21.98 ft

p. 22

1. similar
2. similar
3. neither
4. congruent
5. congruent
6. congruent

Athlete's name: Becky Dyroen-Lancer

p. 23

1. 441 ft²
2. 30 ft²
3. 6500 ft²
4. 162 ft²
5. 702 ft²
6. 45 ft²
7. 50 m²

p. 24

1. 17ft²
2. 12m²
3. 43.4 ft²
4. 3.08 m²
5. 24 ft²
6. 1.35 yd²

7. 60 yd²
8. 90 ft²

p. 25

Message is: GOOD LUCK

p. 26

I.
1. r = 4.25 in, A = 56.72 in²
2. r = 1.91 in, A = 11.46 in²
3. r = .75 in, A = 1.77 in²
4. r = 1.16 in, A = 4.23 in²
5. r = 1.12 in, A = 3.93 in²
6. r = 1.25 in, A = 4.91 in²
7. r = 4.5 in, A = 63.59 in²
8. r = 4 in, A = 50.24 in²
9. r = 1.5 in, A = 7.07 in²

II.
1. basketball
2. soccer ball
3. volleyball
4. women's softball
5. baseball
6. tennis ball
7. men's team handball
8. women's team handball
9. table tennis ball

p. 27

1. 2
2. 4
3. 7
4. 105
5. 9, 11, 12
6. 14, 16, 17
7. 18
8. 60
9. 60
10. 120
11. 19, 20, 21, 23, 25, 27, 29, 31, 32
12. 22, 24, 30

p. 28

1. A
2. C
3. I
4. F
5. B
6. K
7. L
8. H
9. J
10. E
11. G
12. D

p. 29

1. 769.3 cm³
2. 1000 cm³
3. 1125 cm³
4. 1046.86 cm³
5. 301.44 cm³
6. 1099 cm³

7. 753.6 cm³
8. 2064.19 cm³
Figure #3 has the largest capacity.

pp. 30-31

1. 174,375 m³
2. 2,592,100 m³
3. 44,550 m³
4. b
5. a
6. c
7. 70 ft³
8. 60 yd³
9. 160 m³
10. 42.875 m³
11. H

p. 32

1. centimeters
2. meters
3. liter
4. meters
5. kilometers
6. centimeters
7. kilograms
8. centimeters
9. grams
10. centimeters
11. cubic centimeters
12. kiloliters
13. meters
14. no
15. no

p. 33

1. 10,000 mm
2. 354 cm
3. 0.137 km
4. 10,000 cm
5. 1234 cm
6. 100 mm
7. 12,450,000 cm
8. 0.12 cm
9. 45,670 mm
10. 990 m
11. 0.0567 km
12. 0.4567 m
13. 0.569 m
14. 0.9843 m
15. 90 cm
16. 0.456 m
17. 0.00027 cm
18. 87.61 cm
19. 851 m
20. 0.000567 km

pp. 34-35

1. feet
2. feet
3. pounds
4. miles
5. feet

6. inches
7. miles
8. yards
9. ounces
10. inches
11. inches
12. pounds
13. pounds
14. feet or yards
15. pounds
16. miles
17. yards
18. miles
19. pounds
20. feet
21. ounces
22. feet
23. quarts
24. feet or yards

p. 36

1. 35 yards
2. 44 feet
3. 147 pounds
4. 35 minutes
5. 4 inches
6. about 66 ⅔ yards
7. 3 feet
8. 55 feet
9. 27 minutes
10. 16 pounds

p. 37

1. feet
2. second
3. miles
4. miles
5. feet
6. inches
7. inches
8. miles
9. inches
10. ounces
11. feet
12. feet

pp. 38-39

Finished figure should look like this:

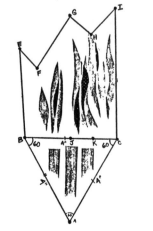

p. 40

Measurements will be approximate. Give credit for answers close to these:
1. A = 60 ft²   P = 32 ft
2. A = 36 ft²   P = 24 ft
3. A = 48 ft²   P = 32 ft
4. A = 36 ft²   P = 24 ft
5. A = 24 ft²   P = 20 ft
6. A = 56 ft²   P = 28 ft
7. A = 15 ft²   P = 18 ft
8. A = 32 ft²   P = 25 ft
9. A = 28 ft²   P = 23 ft
10. A = 104 ft² P = 42 ft

Roomiest Room is # 10

p. 41

1. soccer
2. soccer
3. 25.3 inches
4. about 16.74 inches
5. 11 inches
6. baseball and polo ball
7. basketball
8. about 8.45 ounces
9. 5.25 ounces
10. 21.909 ounces
11.   1. ping pong
      2. tennis
      3. polo
      4. baseball
      5. volleyball
      6. soccer
      7. basketball

p. 42

Answers will be approximate. Give credit for answers close to these measurements.
1. 8400 cm³
2. 9750 cm³
3. 8670 cm³
4. 9000 cm³
5. 7280 cm³
6. 15,000 cm³
7. 9375 cm³
8. 18,630 cm³
9. 10,000 cm³

8 has greatest volume

p. 43

A   1 = 33°
     2 = 105°
     3 = 45°
     4 = 90°
     5 = 25°
     6 = 130°
     7 = 95°
B   8 = 155°
     9 = 30°
   10 = 115°
   11 = 77°
C 12 = 10°

13 = 40°
14 = 88°
15 = 180°

pp. 44-45

1. C
2. B
3. A
4. B
5. B
6. A
7. B
8. C
9. A
10. C
11. B
12. B
13. B
14. A

p. 46

1. 119 lb
2. 130 lb
3. 141 lb
4. 154 lb
5. 167 lb
6. 183 lb
7. 200 lb
8. 218 lb
9. 238 lb
10. 113 kg approx.

p. 47

1. 40° 3F
2. 15° F
3. 48° F
4. 25° F
5. −10° F

p. 48

1. 9.09
2. 10
3. 384
4. 375
5. Measure lines.
6. 440
7. Michael Johnson